HSE
Health & Safety Executive

SUCCESSFUL HEALTH & SAFETY MANAGEMENT

Health and Safety series booklet HS(G) 65

HSE BOOKS

ISBN 0 7176 0425 X

CONTENTS

FOREWORD

This book, by HSE's Accident Prevention Advisory Unit, first published in November 1991, has been well received as providing sound guidance on the practice of health and safety management.

Much of the guidance involves the application of the principles of total quality management (TQM) to health and safety. It has always been true that good health and safety is a part of good management and cannot be achieved without it; TQM takes us further and states the principles that apply to all aspects of management including this one. Since this book first appeared, the Management of Health and Safety at Work Regulations 1992 and the Offshore Installations (Safety Case) Regulations 1992, have come into effect. This revised edition incorporates minor amendments which reflect these important developments as well as the results of an HSE study on the costs of accidents published in January 1993.

The costs of failures in health and safety management are high:
- 30 million days lost in a year from work-related injuries and ill health: nearly ten times the number from strikes;
- a two-thirds increase in real terms of employers' liability insurance costs over the past decade and a doubling of claims since 1985;

The HSE study found:
- uninsured losses from accidents (whether they result in personal injury or not) can cost anything between 8 and 36 times what an organisation normally insures for: in some cases making the difference between profit and loss.

Such losses, whether counted in human or financial terms can for the most part be avoided and the feedback seems to show that real and substantial improvements can be achieved by applying the guidance in this publication. If so, it would appear to be a significant element in any sound business strategy.

The path described is not easy and there are no short cuts. It demands the commitment and involvement of senior management, transmitted down through the line. Modern safety law in effect requires such an approach; but its most attractive aspect is the prospect it offers of replacing the compulsory element in good health and safety standards by approaches based on enlightened self interest and human awareness.

J D RIMINGTON
Director General
Health and Safety Executive

INTRODUCTION

Successful health and safety management has been prepared by HSE's Accident Prevention Advisory Unit (APAU) as a practical guide for directors, managers and health and safety professionals intent on improving health and safety performance. The advice given here will be increasingly used by HSE inspectors as a basis for testing the performance of organisations against the general duties of the Health and Safety at Work etc Act 1974 (HSW Act) and the Management of Health and Safety at Work Regulations 1992 (MHSW).

Organisations which manage health and safety successfully display a number of common characteristics. They have their health and safety risks under control and can demonstrate a progressive improvement in their injury and ill health record. The book describes the principles and health and safety management practices which form the foundations of success of these organisations.

It sets out the issues which need to be addressed and can be used for self audit and assessment and for developing programmes for improvement. Although the principles described are applicable to all organisations, the extent of action required will vary with the size of the organisation, the hazards presented by its activities, products or services and the adequacy of its existing arrangements.

Chapter 1 gives an overview of key issues which need to be considered and which are developed in succeeding chapters. Chapters 2 to 6 are arranged in the following standard form:
- a synopsis of the topics covered in the chapter (blue pages);
- the core material of the chapter. Insets and diagrams are used where necessary to explain important principles;
- a summary at the end of each chapter describing the key ways of controlling that aspect of health and safety management (red pages);
- suggestions for further reading.

Taken together, the chapter summaries describe what organisations aiming to comply with the requirements of Sections 2 to 6 of the HSW Act need to do to manage health and safety effectively. They identify broad areas of competence which need to be developed in ways which are in line with an organisation's own management style and systems.

Many of the features of effective health and safety management are indistinguishable from the sound management practices advocated by proponents of quality and business excellence. Indeed, commercially successful companies often also excel at health and safety management, precisely because they bring efficient business expertise to bear on health and safety as on all other aspects of their operations. The general principles of good management are therefore a sound basis for deciding how to bring about improved health and safety performance.

1
SUMMARY

The key elements of successful health and safety management are set out below, and the relationship between them is outlined in Diagram 1 opposite.

Policy*

Organisations which are successful in achieving high standards of health and safety have health and safety policies which contribute to their business performance, while meeting their responsibilities to people and the environment in a way which fulfils both the spirit and the letter of the law. In this way they satisfy the expectations of shareholders, employees, customers and society at large. Their policies are cost effective and aimed at achieving the preservation and development of physical and human resources and reductions in financial losses and liabilities. Their health and safety policies influence all their activities and decisions, including those to do with the selection of resources and information, the design and operation of working systems, the design and delivery of products and services, and the control and disposal of waste.

Organising*

Organisations which achieve high health and safety standards are structured and operated so as to put their health and safety policies into effective practice. This is helped by the creation of a positive culture which secures involvement and participation at all levels. It is sustained by effective communications and the promotion of competence which enables all employees to make a responsible and informed contribution to the health and safety effort. The visible and active leadership of senior managers is necessary to develop and maintain a culture supportive of health and safety management. Their aim is not simply to avoid accidents, but to motivate and empower people to work safely. The vision, values and beliefs of leaders become the shared 'common knowledge' of all.

Planning*

These successful organisations adopt a planned and systematic approach to policy implementation. Their aim is to minimise the risks* created by work activities, products and services. They use risk assessment methods to decide priorities and set objectives for hazard* elimination and risk reduction. Performance standards are established and performance is measured against them. Specific actions needed to promote a positive health and safety culture and to eliminate and control risks are identified. Wherever possible, risks are eliminated by the careful selection and design of facilities, equipment and processes or minimised by the use of physical control measures. Where this is not possible systems of work and personal protective equipment are used to control risks.

Measuring performance*

Health and safety performance in organisations which manage health and safety successfully, is measured against pre-determined standards. This reveals when and where action is needed to improve performance. The success of action taken to control risks is assessed through active self-monitoring involving a range of techniques. This includes an examination of both hardware (premises, plant and substances) and software (people, procedures and systems), including individual behaviour. Failures of control are assessed through reactive monitoring which requires the thorough investigation of any accidents, ill health or incidents* with the potential to cause harm or loss. In both active and reactive monitoring the objectives are not only to determine the immediate causes of sub-standard performance but, more importantly, to identify the underlying causes and the implications for the design and operation of the health and safety management system.

Auditing* and reviewing* performance

Learning from **all** relevant experience and applying the lessons learned, are important elements in effective health and safety management. This needs to be done systematically through regular reviews of performance based on data both from monitoring activities and from independent audits of the whole health and safety management system. These form the basis for self-regulation and for securing compliance with Sections 2 to 6 of the Health and Safety at Work etc Act 1974. Commitment to continuous improvement involves the constant development of policies, approaches to implementation and techniques of risk control. Organisations which achieve high standards of health and safety assess their health and safety performance by internal reference to key performance indicators and by external comparison with the performance of business competitors. They often also record and account for their performance in their annual reports.

* For definitions see Appendix 1

Diagram 1   Key elements of successful health and safety management

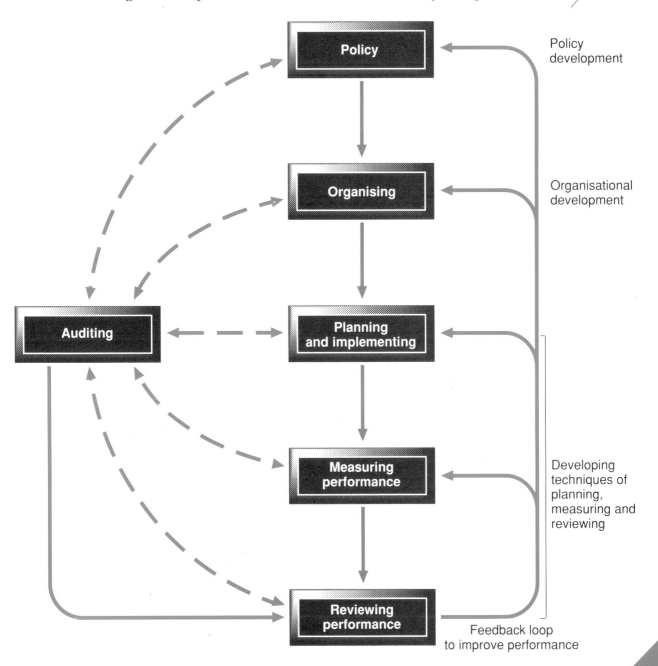

EFFECTIVE HEALTH AND SAFETY POLICIES

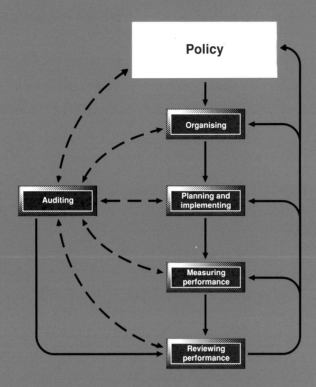

Synopsis

This chapter outlines the characteristics of effective health and safety policies and demonstrates how they can contribute to business performance by:

- supporting human resource development;

- minimising the financial losses which arise from avoidable unplanned events;

- recognising that accidents, ill health and incidents result from failings in management control and are not just the fault of individual employees;

- recognising that the development of a culture supportive of health and safety is necessary to achieve adequate control over risks;

- ensuring a systematic approach to the identification of risks and the allocation of resources to control them; and

- supporting quality initiatives aimed at continuous improvement.

EFFECTIVE HEALTH AND SAFETY POLICIES

The health and safety policies adopted by organisations achieving high standards of health and safety display a number of common characteristics which reflect the values and beliefs of those who devise and implement them. This chapter identifies the main characteristics of successful policies. Each section includes statements which aim to sum up the beliefs which underlie each characteristic. These statements are typical of the views expressed by these successful organisations.

The importance of people to the organisation

Work can make a positive or a negative contribution to a person's health. When people are exposed to danger (for example, in the form of exposure to chemicals, certain repetitive tasks or a risk of falling) physical and mental health may suffer. In the absence of danger, when people are interested and involved in their work, satisfaction and enjoyment are increased and improvements in health and wellbeing can result. This spectrum is illustrated in Diagram 2.

Underlying belief

people

are our most

important

asset

The activities of organisations successful in health and safety management recognise this relationship between controlling risks and general health. Their health and safety policies are aligned with other human resource management policies designed to secure the commitment, involvement and wellbeing of employees. This includes things such as the restructuring of jobs to reduce monotony and increase flexibility, and health promotion campaigns which encourage healthy eating and exercise. In some cases organisations educate their employees about dangers in the home as part as an off-the-job accident prevention policy.

The best health and safety policies are concerned not only with preventing injury and ill health* (as required by health and safety legislation), but also with positive health promotion which gives practical expression to the belief that people

INSET 1

ACCIDENT RATIO STUDIES

Several studies have been undertaken to establish the relationship between serious and minor accidents and other dangerous events. The results of three such studies are summarised here. The most significant conclusions which can be drawn from this research are that:

• although the detailed findings of the studies were different because of the definitions and accident data used, each study demonstrates a consistent relationship between the different kinds of event. There are consistently greater numbers of less serious events taking place than the more serious events;

• as it was often a matter of chance whether dangerous events caused ill health, injury or damage, the 'no injury' incidents or 'near misses' in each case had the potential to become events with more serious consequences. However, not all near misses involve risks which might have caused fatal or serious injury;

• **all** the events (not just those causing injuries) represent failures in control and were therefore potential learning experiences through which improved control could have been established;

• effective health and safety policies will therefore have to examine **all** unsafe events and the behaviours which give rise to them, both as a means of establishing control and as a means of measuring. performance.

APAU (1993)
From costings studies in five organisations in the oil, food, construction, health and transport sectors, APAU established the following ratio:

1 major or over-3-day lost time injury
7 minor injuries
189 non-injury accidents
(The costs of accidents at work
HS(G)96 see reference 11, page 14.)

* For definition see Appendix 1

are a key resource. They recognise that progressive human resource management policies can be undermined by weak health and safety policies. The provision of more rewarding and satisfying jobs will not convince people that management are concerned for their wellbeing if injuries and ill health continue to be a by-product of those jobs.

The ultimate goal is an organisation in which accidents and ill health are eliminated, and in which work forms part of a satisfying life, contributing to physical and mental wellbeing, to the benefit of both the individual and the organisation. This reflects not only a desire to behave ethically and responsibly, but also a recognition of the positive benefits which can accrue from a fit, enthusiastic, competent and committed workforce.

This integrated approach, in which the needs of people and the prosperity of the organisation go hand in hand, extends to people outside the organisation, in policies for the control of off-site risks, environmental pollution and product safety.

Avoiding loss - The total loss approach

Underlying belief

the preservation of human and physical resources is an important means of minimising costs

The costs of injuries and ill health are only one component of unwanted happenings which result in unnecessary financial losses. Accidental damage to property, plant or products also imposes costs. The lower half of Diagram 2 (page 8) outlines the range of losses and the potential benefits of good loss control.

Under the total loss approach, accidents are taken to include not only those circumstances which actually cause ill health or injury, but also every event involving damage to property, plant, products or the environment, production losses, or increased liabilities. The total loss approach is based on research into accident causation which is summarised in Inset 1. This indicates that there are many more

OUTLINE OF THREE ACCIDENT RATIO STUDIES

Bird (1969)

From an analysis of 1 753 498 accidents reported by 297 co-operating organisations in the USA, representing 21 different types of occupational establishment and employing 1 750 000 people who worked more than 3 billion man hours during the exposure period analysed, F E Bird Jnr drew up the following ratio:

1 serious or disabling injury
10 minor injuries (any reported injury less than serious)
30 property damage accidents (all types)
600 incidents with no visible injury or damage.
(*Practical loss control leadership* - F E Bird Jnr and G L Germain 1985.)

Tye/Pearson (1974/75)

Based on a study of almost 1 000 000 accidents in British industry Tye and Pearson drew up the following ratio:

1 fatal or serious injury
3 minor injuries - when the victim would be absent for up to 3 days
50 injuries requiring first-aid treatment
80 property damage accidents
400 non-injury/damage incidents or 'near misses'
(*Management safety manual* - British Safety Council 5-Star Health and Safety Management System.)

Diagram 2 Spectrum of occupational health

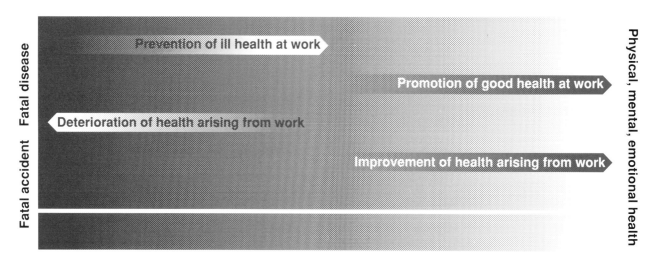

Losses expressed by:
Ill health and injuries,
Damage to property, plant, products and
the environment,
Loss to process and increased liabilities.

Positive benefits expressed by:
Reduced absenteeism,
Improved job satisfaction,
General health and efficiency arising
from increased commitment
co-operation and competence.

'incidents' or near-miss events than those which cause injury or property damage. The examination of the causes of all such loss events can provide valuable insights into inadequacies in risk control and action which could prevent future injuries or losses. For example, if a man slips on a patch of spilled oil, he may be unhurt, he may damage clothing or equipment, he may break his arm or he may fracture his skull and die. Effective prevention and loss control must focus on the **cause** of the accident not its results. The consequences of accidents are often matters of chance over which there can be little control.

INSET 2

HUMAN FACTORS IN INDUSTRIAL SAFETY

The diagram illustrates the relationship between the three factors which influence behaviour in organisations.

Organisational factors have the major influence on individual and group behaviour, yet it is not uncommon for aspects of the organisation's influence to be overlooked during the design of work and in the investigation of accidents and incidents. Organisations need to establish their own positive safety culture and a climate which promotes employee involvement and commitment at all levels, emphasising that deviation from established safety standards is unacceptable.

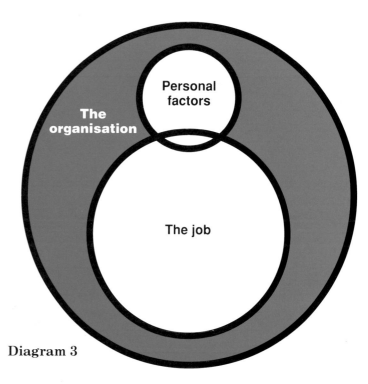

Diagram 3

The total loss approach therefore emphasises learning from both accidents **and** incidents to achieve effective control. It involves drawing lessons both from within the organisation (including all sites) and from other organisations. The emphasis is on preventing accidents by identifying risks and the sources of potential ill health, injury or loss. Investment in the reduction of losses contributes directly to profits and is cost effective, particularly at times of high competition when it may yield a better return than a similar investment to improve sales and market share. A number of organisations have publicly stated their belief in the cost effectiveness of their accident prevention and health promotion strategies (see references 8, 9 and 10, page 14). Results from studies of the costs of accidental loss recently undertaken by APAU confirm their commercial significance (see reference 11, page 14).

Accidents are caused by the absence of adequate management control

Accidents, ill health and incidents are seldom inevitable random events. They generally arise from failures in control and often have multiple causes. Although the immediate cause of an event may be a human or technical failure, such events usually arise from organisational failings which are the responsibility of management. Successful policies place heavy emphasis on achieving effective control over both people and technology. They aim to exploit the strengths of employees while minimising the influence of human limitations and fallibilities through the way the organisation is structured and the way jobs and systems are designed.

Underlying belief

the majority of accidents

and incidents are

not caused by

'careless workers',

but by failures in control

(either within the organisation

or within the particular job),

which are the responsibility

of management

Critical to this approach is an understanding of how 'human factors' affect health and safety performance. This is explained in the Health and Safety Executive publication, *Human factors in industrial safety*, which also contains guidance on the development of suitable control strategies based on a systematic approach (see reference 3, page 14). There are three key areas of influence on behaviour - the organisation, the job and the person - see Inset 2.

Job factors directly influence individual performance and the control of risks. Tasks should be designed according to ergonomic principles to take account of the limitations of human performance. Mismatches between job requirements and individuals' capabilities increase the potential for human error. Matching the job to the individual ensures that people are not overloaded and this contributes to consistent performance. Physical matching includes how the whole workplace and the working environment are designed. Mental matching involves taking into account the individuals information and decision-making requirements as well as their perception of the task. Mismatches between job requirements and individuals capabilities increase the potential for human error.

Personal factors - the attributes which employees bring to their jobs - may be strengths or weaknesses in relation to the demands of a particular task. They include both physical attributes (such as strength and limitations arising from disability or illness) and mental attributes such as habits, attitudes, skills and personality which influence behaviour in complex ways. Negative effects on task performance cannot always be mitigated by job design solutions. Some characteristics such as skills and attitudes, are amenable to modification or enhancement through training and experience; others, such as personality, are relatively permanent and incapable of modification within the work context. People may therefore need to be matched to their jobs through appropriate selection techniques.

* From *Human factors in industrial safety*
(see reference 3, page 14).

The importance of organisational factors

The creation of an effective organisation for health and safety is central to the successful management of risks and the reduction of injuries, ill health and losses. It should be designed to maximise the contribution of individuals and groups through participation at all levels. A positive health and safety culture needs to be

Underlying beliefs

health and safety is a management responsibility of equal importance to production and quality

.

effective control of health and safety is achieved through co-operative effort at all levels in the organisation

effective health and safety management is not 'common sense' but is based on a common understanding of risks and how to control them brought about through good management

.

competence in managing health and safety is an essential part of professional management

developed in which health and safety objectives are regarded by all as aligned to other business goals. This can only happen through the active and continued commitment of senior managers and directors who, in their individual behaviour and management practice, effectively communicate the beliefs which underlie the health and safety policy. Health and safety is regarded as a boardroom issue, with a board member taking direct responsibility for the co-ordination of effort. The whole organisation comes to share management's perception and beliefs about the importance of health and safety and the need to achieve the policy objectives which have been established and communicated.

A systematic approach

Planning is critical to effective policy implementation. The aim is to apply the logic and rigour of business planning to the identification and control of risks. Analysis and appropriate procedures ensure the systematic identification of risks and the establishment of objectives and performance standards. Risk assessment techniques enable resources to be properly allocated and priorities for action to be set. Structured monitoring arrangements allow performance against plans to be measured objectively.

Underlying belief

all accidents, ill health and incidents are preventable

Organisations achieving high standards of health and safety spend more resources on the control of health and safety risks than the average, but consider that this expenditure is cost effective in terms of improved performance. The extent to which health and safety thinking is reflected in business activity and decision making is an important determinant of effectiveness. The practical implications of health and safety policies are thought through so as to avoid conflict between the demands of policy and other operational requirements. The consequences of failing to do so are illustrated in the extreme case by disasters such as the sinking of the Herald of Free Enterprise, the train crash at Clapham Junction and the fire and explosion on Piper Alpha. In these cases management decisions where insufficient attention or weight was given to health and safety led to:

- unrealistic timescales for the implementation of plans which put pressure on people to cut corners and reduce supervision;
- work scheduling and rosters which failed to take account of the problems of

fatigue;
- inadequate resources being allocated to training;
- organisational restructuring which placed people in positions for which they had insufficient experience;
- jobs and control systems which failed to recognise or allow for the fact that people were likely to make mistakes and might have difficulties communicating with each other.

An outline of how effective health and safety policies should impact on various aspects of business thinking is given in Inset 3.

An outline of how effective health and safety policies should impact on various aspects of business thinking is given in Inset 3.

INSET 3

THE IMPACT OF EFFECTIVE HEALTH AND SAFETY POLICIES ON BUSINESS THINKING

The following areas of business thinking are amongst those which are influenced by effective health and safety policies:

Corporate strategy and social responsibility
- business mission, philosophy and codes of ethics;
- company image in the community;
- policy on environmental impact;
- management professionalism (for example, the application of the Management Charter Initiative (MCI) competences).

Finance
- loss control and cost reduction strategies;
- aspects of non-speculative risk management, such as product liability, security, property damage, and the consequential potential for financial loss and legal liability;
- decisions on loss reduction, risk retention or transfer, risk funding and insurance;
- investment decisions concerning business acquisitions and new premises, plant and processes;
- general financial planning and budgetary control.

Human resources
- recruitment, selection, placement, transfer, training, development and learning;
- structuring of the organisation to promote a positive health and safety culture;
- work and job structuring to achieve participation and involvement;
- health promotion activities;
- communications.

Marketing, product design and product liability
- specification of product and service health and safety standards;
- national legal requirements, for example, Section 6 of the Health and Safety at Work etc Act 1974;
- international requirements such as EC directives;
- national and international consensus standards, for example, British Standards, ANSI and ISO Standards;
- the Consumer Protection Act in the case of products for domestic use.

Manufacturing and operating policy
- design/selection/construction/ maintenance of premises, plant, equipment and substances;
- design of jobs and the application of ergonomic principles and appropriate strategies for risk elimination, reduction and control;
- quality management;
- environmental management and waste disposal.

Information management and systems
- the identification of data critical to the management of health and safety;
- the selection of appropriate performance indicators;
- the use of information technology in the collection and analysis of essential data.

Another essential element of the systematic approach is commitment to continuous improvement. Striving to improve the health and safety management system is an important element in the improvement and maintenance of high standards. Learning from experience is essential. Failure to do so can lead to tragedy, as illustrated in the Clapham and Herald of Free Enterprise disasters mentioned earlier. In each case previous incidents had given warning of the potential for serious injury. Experience should influence the development of both policies and more effective techniques of implementation. This requires regular detailed reviews of performance against plans, and regular audits of the whole health and safety management system.

Safety and quality

There are considerable similarities between the approaches to health and safety described in this chapter and those advocated for effective quality management. The adoption of quality management systems will not automatically lead to high standards of health and safety in all areas (for example, compliance with British Standard 5750 should lead to the manufacture of products which are free from health and safety risks, but will not necessarily lead to good standards of health and safety in the production process). The principles of good health and safety management and good quality management are, however, the same.

> Underlying belief
> *health and safety,*
> *and quality,*
> *are two sides*
> *of the*
> *same coin*

There is increasing recognition that a developed approach to quality is an essential feature of a successful organisation, not an optional extra. The emphasis is on 'managing quality in' rather than 'inspecting defects out'. Those organisations which have adopted this approach and applied it to their health and safety management systems, often as part of a total quality management (TQM) philosophy, achieve particularly high standards of health and safety performance.

The TQM approach seeks to promote continuous improvement in all aspects of an organisation's activities. As the term 'total quality' would imply, the ultimate goal for health and safety is an injury-free working environment, and this is the target which a number of organisations have set themselves. Such organisations are not acting out of purely philanthropic motives. They have clearly recognised that accidents and ill health cost money and that an effective system for managing health and safety will help reduce what in quality terms is known as the 'cost of non-conformance'.

Success in quality management requires the development of supportive organisational cultures. The TQM philosophy stresses the importance of the active involvement of all employees in the quality process. Organisations which are successful in the management of health and safety go to great lengths to develop a positive safety culture on the same basis.

In the chapters which follow, the similarities and strong links between total quality management and effective health and safety management will become increasingly apparent. Readers whose organisations are already committed to TQM will find that the recommended approaches are not unfamiliar and should be able to see how they could readily be adopted within their organisation.

EFFECTIVE HEALTH AND SAFETY POLICIES
SUMMARY

Effective health and safety management demands comprehensive health and safety policies which fulfil the spirit and the letter of the law, which are effectively implemented and which are considered in all business practice and decision making.

Organisations achieving high standards of health and safety develop policies which recognise:

- that health and safety can contribute to business performance by preserving and developing human and physical resources, by reducing costs and liabilities and as means of expressing corporate responsibility;

- that leaders must develop appropriate organisational structures and a culture which supports risk control and secures the full participation of all members of the organisation;

- the need to resource and plan policy implementation adequately;

- that the only effective approach to injury, ill health and loss prevention is one based on the systematic identification and control of risk;

- the need for the organisation to develop an understanding of risk control and to be responsive to internal and external change;

- the need to scrutinise and review performance so as to learn from experience;

- the connection between quality and health and safety.

FURTHER READING

1 CBI *Developing a safety culture: Business for safety* 1990 ISBN 0 85201 361 2

2 Bird FE and Germain GL *Practical loss control leadership* International Loss Control Institute 1986 Loganville, Georgia, Institute Publishing ISBN 0 88061 054 9

3 HSE *Human factors in industrial safety* HS(G) 48 HMSO 1989 ISBN 0 11 885486 0

4 *A manager's guide to reducing human errors: improving human performance in the chemical industry* 1990 Chemical Manufacturers Association Inc, 2501 M Street NW, Washington DC 20037

5 *Managing occupational health and safety (OHS)* Management Checklist No H3 British Institute of Management 1990

6 HSE Accident Prevention Advisory Unit *The management of health and safety* Industrial Society Notes for managers series 1988 ISBN 0 85 290409 6

7 Jardine Insurance Brokers Ltd *Risk management - practical techniques to minimise exposure to accidental losses* 2nd edition Kogan Page 1988 ISBN 1 85091 351 X

8 Dees JP and Taylor R Health care management: a tool for the future *American Association of Occupational Health Nurses Journal* Feb 1990 Vol 38 No 2 52-58

9 Crunk J *Safety at DuPont, a cost benefit study* via: DuPont De Nemours (Deutschland) Gmbh, Safety Management Services, Europe Postfach 1393, 4700 Hamm 1

10 Witter RE Safety program payoff *Plant Operations Progress* July 1982 Vol 1 No 3 139-141

11 HSE *The costs of accidents at work* HS(G)96, HMSO 1993, ISBN 0 11 886374 6

12 HSC Advisory Committee on Safety of Nuclear Installations *Study group on human factors - third report on organising for safety* HMSO 1993 ISBN 0 11 882104 0

3

ORGANISING FOR HEALTH AND SAFETY

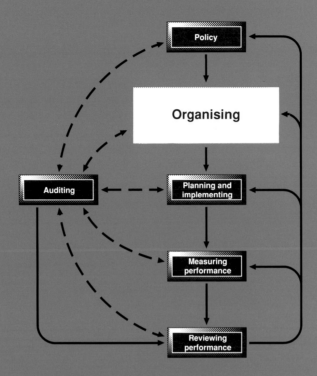

Synopsis

Organising for health and safety involves establishing responsibilities and relationships which promote a positive health and safety culture and secure the implementation and continued development of the health and safety policy. This chapter examines the characteristics of structures and processes which:

- establish and maintain management **control** within an organisation;

- promote **co-operation** between individuals, safety representatives and groups so that health and safety becomes a collaborative effort;

- ensure the **communication** of necessary information throughout the organisation; and

- secure the **competence** of employees.

ORGANISING FOR HEALTH AND SAFETY

Organising for health and safety is the process of designing and establishing the responsibilities and relationships which form the social environment in which work takes place. The influence of an organisation's culture bears on all aspects of work activity, affecting individual and group behaviour, job design and the planning and execution of work.

A culture which promotes safe and healthy working is therefore crucial to the proper implementation and continued development of effective policies. Such cultures take time to mature and, typically, five to ten years to consolidate, but they are an essential means of influencing the behaviour of individuals. Each organisation will have a distinctive approach to health and safety which is shared 'common knowledge' and which promotes a common way of thinking about and responding to health and safety issues. Organisations should aim to develop a positive health and safety culture.

In this chapter the activities necessary to promote positive health and safety cultures have been categorised into four separate elements. These are concerned with:
- methods of **control** within the organisation;
- the means of securing **co-operation** between individuals, safety representatives and groups;
- the methods of **communication** throughout the organisation;
- the **competence** of individuals.

Control is the foundation of a positive health and safety culture and the management techniques used by those in positions of control are considered in more detail in chapters 4 to 6. All four elements are, however, inter-related and inter-dependent so that, for example, action taken to achieve control, competence and co-operation all communicate management's intention and commitment. Consistent activity in each area is necessary to promote a climate in which a positive health and safety culture can develop and targets can be achieved.

CONTROL

In organisations achieving success in health and safety, control is achieved by securing the commitment of employees to clear health and safety objectives. Managers take full responsibility for controlling all those factors which could lead to ill health, injury or loss. They provide clear direction and take responsibility for the working environment in which accidents, ill health and incidents could occur. This creates a positive atmosphere and encourages a creative and learning culture in which the emphasis is on a collective effort to develop and maintain systems of control before the event rather than on blaming individuals for failures afterwards.

Establishing and maintaining control is central to all management functions including health and safety. Organisations achieving high standards of health and safety allocate health and safety responsibilities to line managers, while specialists act as advisers. A senior figure at the top of the organisation is nominated to co-ordinate and monitor policy implementation.

The key functions of successful health and safety management can be classified into three broad areas. These are:
- formulating and developing policy and the organisation, which includes

identifying key health and safety objectives and reviewing progress towards their achievement;

- planning, measuring, reviewing and auditing health and safety activities so that legal requirements are satisfied and all risks are minimised;
- ensuring effective implementation of plans and reporting on performance.

Further details about these three functions are given in Appendix 2.

These functions may be performed by the same individuals or groups, although it is important when specifying and documenting duties and responsibilities, to establish the precise nature of the functions which are to be performed and the boundaries of discretion. Effectiveness is promoted by the clear definition of responsibilities and co-ordination to ensure that individual contributions support the achievement of the policy objectives, that no key tasks are overlooked, and that duplication of effort is avoided. The clarification of responsibilities is particularly important where two or more organisations work together, for example, when contractors are employed to provide goods or services within an existing establishment.

Organisations successful in health and safety management describe their policy arrangements and organisational structure for health and safety in written statements. Additionally, directives and performance standards are used to define in detail who should do what, when, and to specify the results required. Performance standards link responsibilities to desired outputs and recognise that the achievement of goals is always based on specific work, the nature of which is defined and the effects of which are measured. Where necessary, the work input may be further defined by written systems, rules or procedures which clarify the processes by which jobs and tasks should be performed in order to achieve the desired results. Guidelines on drawing up performance standards are given in Inset 4. Defining performance standards is an important part of planning and measuring health and safety activities and is considered in more detail in chapter 4.

PERFORMANCE STANDARDS

INSET 4

Performance standards are the basis for planning and measuring health and safety achievement. They reflect the fact that the attainment of objectives requires the input of specific effort. If organisations are to be efficient and effective in controlling risks they need to co-ordinate activities and ensure that everyone is clear about what they are expected to achieve. They need to understand and specify what has to be done, from controlling the direction of the organisation as a whole to dealing with the specific risks created by different activities, products or services.

Setting performance standards is one of the cornerstones of the effective implementation of health and safety policies. Policy is translated from good intentions into a series of co-ordinated activities and tasks which:

- set out clearly what people need to do to contribute to an environment free of injuries, ill health and loss;
- assist in identifying the competences which individuals need to fulfil their responsibilities;

- form the basis for measuring individual, group and organisational performance.

Performance standards link responsibilities to desired outputs and should specify who is responsible, for what and with what expected result. They should be devised for all work relevant to health and safety, including the work of managers (at **all** levels) and other employees. A performance standard should generally cover the following:

- **Who is responsible?** The standards should identify the name or position of those with responsibility for carrying out the work, providing the detail necessary to support general organisational statements.
  Consideration should be given in all cases to the competence criteria for doing the work.

- **What for?** The standards should identify what is to be done and explain how. This may involve the application of specific procedures or systems of work (legally prescribed or otherwise) and the use of ▶

17

The clear definition of responsibilities is reinforced by holding individuals accountable for their responsibilities. This often involves the use of supporting systems and arrangements, such as:

- reference to health and safety responsibilities in individual job descriptions;
- formal performance review and appraisal systems which include the measuring and rewarding of individual performance in health and safety related activities;
- procedures which identify and take action on failures to achieve adequate health and safety performance and which apply equally to managers and other employees. Such procedures can be integrated with normal disciplinary arrangements and be invoked when justified by the seriousness of the failure to comply.

The health and safety performance of individuals, particularly supervisors and managers, is closely monitored and is a determinant in career progession and personal development assessments. Health and safety objectives are regarded as being of equal importance to other business aims, and individual health and safety targets are agreed to secure commitment to their achievement. The emphasis is on identifying what needs to be done in order to prevent injuries, ill health and loss. Performance standards form the basis for the objective measurement and assessment of individual performance. Such standards are also used to measure group and organisational performance.

A combination of rewards and sanctions is used to motivate all employees. More emphasis is, however, placed on the reinforcement of the positive behaviour which contributes to risk control and the promotion of a positive safety culture. The general payment and reward systems support the achievement of health and safety objectives and avoid conflict with output and other commercial objectives. Where safety award schemes are used, these emphasise the attainment of specific standards

 ▶ specific documents and equipment. Some examples of what is to be done might be:

- drawing up plans at various levels to implement the health and safety policy;
- carrying out assessments in accordance with the Control of Substances Hazardous to Health Regulations 1988 (COSHH) before hazardous substances are used;
- the periodic monitoring of health and safety performance;
- checking contractors' health and safety performance before awarding contracts;
- the holding by supervisors of weekly 'tool-box' talks with their team on health and safety issues. ('Tool-box' talks, or 'tailgate' meetings, are planned regular meetings where supervisors discuss with their team a specific health and safety issue or topic.) This may include, for example, a reminder of important safety procedures or the lessons from a recent accident;
- providing training in accordance with the Woodworking Machines Regulations 1974 before employees are allowed to operate a circular saw;

- taking the steps necessary to comply with Section 30 of the Factories Act 1961 before entering a confined space;
- providing first aid after an accident.

- **When?** The standards should specify when the work is to be carried out. This may be on a regular basis (eg monthly inspections by supervisors or managers) or only when particular tasks or jobs are done (eg when using a ladder or a particular chemical).

- **With what expected result?** The standards for outputs may be specified by reference to specific legal requirements. They may alternatively be in terms of the satisfactory completion of specified procedures (eg the completion of reports following an inspection or the completion of a training procedure). Output standards can be used to specify how individuals are to be held accountable for their health and safety responsibilities. The quantity and quality of outputs can be used to measure personal, group or corporate performance.

of performance rather than arbitrary targets or those based solely on the avoidance of accidents or ill health. The best schemes reward group rather than individual effort and support the collaborative approach to health and safety management. Effective supervision is of critical importance and further guidance on this is contained in Inset 5.

SUPERVISION

Adequate supervision complements the provision of information, instruction and training in ensuring that the health and safety policy of an organisation is effectively implemented and developed. Supervision has two key aspects:

• **Task management.** The primary task is to ensure the achievement of specific health and safety objectives and safe working in accordance with performance standards. This involves the provision of direction, help, guidance, example and discipline, with the aim of ensuring that risks are fully understood and performance standards and supporting procedures and systems are consistently applied. Effective task management also involves local planning to achieve objectives; training and coaching in skills to develop individual competence; and monitoring to identify any existing performance standards which are inappropriate or inadequate and require revision. It involves both the use of formal monitoring systems and general monitoring through spot checks and continuous observation.

• **Team building** in which the supervisor encourages individuals to work together in pursuit of team health and safety objectives. The supervisor's role includes the leading of team activities such as 'tool-box' talks, team briefings, and problem solving exercises. It involves coaching and counselling to encourage and support the participation of all team members. A particularly important objective is to secure a growth in understanding of the risks involved in the work of the group and how these can be either eliminated or better controlled.

Levels of supervision need to be the subject of positive management consideration and decision making. The appropriate level depends on the risks involved and on the competence of employees to identify and handle them. In some cases legal requirements stipulate the supervision of certain activities, eg in factories young people working at certain dangerous machines have to be supervised by an experienced person until they have received sufficient training. Employees new to a job, undergoing training, doing jobs which present special risks, or dealing with new situations may need more supervision than others. Some supervision of fully competent individuals will, however, always be required to ensure that standards are being consistently met. ▶

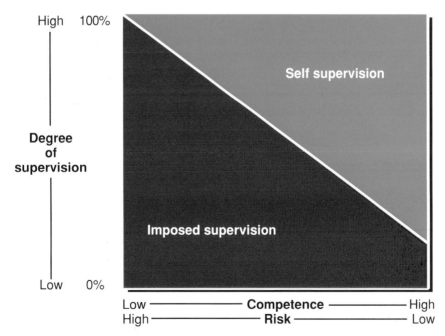

Diagram 4 Levels of supervision
Levels of supervision are determined by the risk of the job and the competence of the person

► Health and safety supervision should not be reactive, involving only responses to requests for help. Supervisory regimes should be designed and organised as part of a proper system of active management control. Particular attention should be given to the problems of people working alone, job sharing and part-time working, and continuity at shift change-overs.

Supervisors and employees need to exercise judgement and discretion, for example, when making decisions on when to seek help or guidance, when to report hazards, or when to halt work because they consider it too dangerous to continue. They should, however, exercise this discretion within the framework of control established at the top of the organisation. Although authority to act can be delegated to supervisors and individual employees, the ultimate responsibility for complying with the employer's legal duties cannot be delegated. It follows that management must ensure that those exercising discretion and judgement are competent to do so and have clear guidelines.

A growing number of organisations are developing new methods of team working which are often linked to the widening of job content and to flexible working. This can mean, for example, that:

- some maintenance tasks become the responsibility of the work group, which may involve some maintenance workers joining production teams;
- job variety for individuals is increased and they have to become competent in new tasks;
- supervisors become responsible for areas of work which are not within their established expertise or experience.

In some cases the formal supervisory role may not be defined and 'team leaders' may be allowed to emerge naturally or be elected by group members. There may also be a policy that there should be a minimum of direct supervision so that the groups are encouraged to identify and solve their own problems.

Such initiatives can have positive benefits if group performance criteria covers health and safety. However, the health and safety implications need to be carefully considered, with specific steps being taken to deal with them. Team and flexible working usually increase the discretion available to supervisors and others. In situations where supervisors acquire wider responsibilities they need to become familiar with new risks and with how these relate to the activities of the whole group and of other groups. Increasing the discretion and responsibilities of supervisors and others therefore needs to be accompanied by sufficient training and experience to develop their competence in the exercise of the relevant health and safety judgements.

CO-OPERATION

Participation, commitment and involvement in health and safety activities at all levels is essential, not only to fulfil legal obligations for consultation, but also to achieve effective risk control. Pooling knowledge and experience is a key aspect of risk control. Participation complements control in that it encourages the 'ownership' of health and safety policies by employees at all levels, and establishes an understanding that the organisation as a whole and those working in it benefit from good health and safety performance. Health and safety really does become 'everybody's business'.

Health and safety committees and similar consultative bodies are used as a means of securing formal participation in the control of the health and safety effort. Safety representatives are provided with paid time off for specialist training and adequate facilities on site. This satisfies the minimum legal requirements for co-operation and participation laid down in Sections 2(6) and 2(7) of the Health and Safety at Work etc Act 1974, the Safety Representatives and Safety Committees Regulations 1977 and the Offshore Installations (Safety Representatives & Safety Committee) Regulations 1989.

However, successful organisations are not satisfied with mere legal compliance and they **actively encourage and support safety representatives** in their role, recognising the valuable contribution they can make. Safety representatives are provided with training which, in common with all employees, enables them to make an informed contribution on health and safety issues. They also enjoy the positive benefits of an open communications policy and are also closely involved in directing the health and safety effort by the nature of the issues discussed at health and safety committees. Effective consultative bodies are involved in planning, measuring and reviewing performance as well as in their more traditional reactive role of considering the results of accident, ill health and incident investigations and other concerns of the moment.

In organisations achieving success in health and safety, employees at all levels are also involved in groups concerned with setting performance standards, devising operational systems, procedures and instructions for the control of risks and with monitoring and auditing activities. The involvement of supervisors and others in writing systems and procedures is particularly important. Reference to their intimate knowledge of how work is done is essential if procedures are to be relevant, accepted and written in a form which can be applied in practice. Such arrangements secure the effective participation of employees in safety policy formulation and development. In some cases *ad hoc* problem solving teams brought together from various parts of the organisation can help solve specific problems, including issues which may have arisen from an accident, a case of ill health or an incident. All these group activities have the support of management and access to advice from health and safety specialists.

Other approaches to promote involvement include the use of hazard report books, suggestion schemes, or safety circles (similar to quality circles), where safety problems are identified and solved. These too can help to develop enthusiasm and enable useful expertise and knowledge to be drawn upon.

The involvement of employees may, in the short term, increase the potential for conflict and disagreement about what constitutes safe and healthy working. The activities of supervisors and managers need therefore to be supported by procedures which establish when and how specialist advice can be obtained to resolve problems and disputes, when a specific investigation should be made, and the circumstances in which work should be suspended. In the longer term the potential for conflict is reduced as the participants develop constructive working relationships and shared objectives.

COMMUNICATION

Effective communication is essential. This involves information coming into the organisation, flowing within the organisation and going out from the organisation.

Information inputs to the organisation

Good sources of 'health and safety intelligence' coming into the organisation are as important for the development of health and safety policy and performance as market information is for business development. Such information is particularly necessary for those responsible for policy making, planning, setting performance standards, measuring, auditing and reviewing performance. Arrangements are necessary to monitor legal developments with which the organisation may need to comply; technical developments which might be relevant to risk control; and developments in health and safety management practice.

Information flows within the organisation

Effective internal communication is essential if the health and safety policy is to be understood and consistently implemented. Systems are also needed to communicate key information such as:

- the meaning and purpose of the policy;
- the vision, values and beliefs which underlie it;
- the commitment of senior management to its implementation;
- plans, standards, procedures and systems relating to implementation and performance measurement;
- factual information which will help secure the involvement and commitment of work people (including relevant information from outside services);
- comments and ideas for improvement from individuals and groups;
- reports on performance.

A comprehensive system is made up of a variety of formal and informal means of communication which together ensure an adequate flow of information up, down and across the organisation. Organisations successful in health and safety make full use of three inter-related methods: visible behaviour by managers and others; the written word; and face-to-face discussion. The content of all three methods needs to be consistent and should be co-ordinated so as to reinforce key messages. These organisations also adopt open information policies, in some cases providing libraries or information rooms to which all employees have access.

Visible behaviour

Leading by example, is essential in promoting a positive health and safety culture. The visible demonstration by managers, and particularly by senior managers, of the importance and significance of health and safety objectives communicates powerful signals. Managers also need to be aware of the negative effect of behaviour which

EXAMPLES OF STATEMENTS OF HEALTH AND SAFETY PHILOSOPHY

INSET 6

"A good safety record goes hand in hand with high productivity and quality standards."

"We believe that an excellent company is by definition a safe company. Since we are committed to excellence it follows that minimising risk to people, plant and products is inseparable from all other company objectives."

"Experience shows that a successful safety organisation also produces the right quality goods at minimum costs."

**"Prevention is not only better, but cheaper than cure ...
There is no necessary conflict between humanitarianism and commercial considerations.
Profits and safety are not in competition.
On the contrary, safety is good business."**

**"Total safety is the ongoing integration of safety into all activities with the objective of attaining industry leadership in safety performance.
We believe:
Nothing is more important than safety
... not production, not sales, not profits."**

The Health and Safety Executive wish to thank the five companies who have allowed us to quote their views.

suggests insincerity, and effort needs to be put into maintaining consistency between what is said and what is done. Amongst the methods which successful companies use to signal commitment are:

- regular 'health and safety tours' by managers, including, when appropriate, senior managers, planned so as progressively to cover the whole site or operation. Such tours are not detailed inspections but are designed to demonstrate management commitment and interest and to enable them to see for themselves obvious examples of good or bad performance. They can also focus attention on current priorities in the overall safety effort.

- the chairing of meetings of the central health and safety committee or other joint consultative body being the regular responsibility of a member of top management.

- managers becoming actively involved in accident, ill health and incident investigations, with the level of seniority being determined by the severity of the event and their involvement extending to the collection of information and the interviewing of witnesses.

Written communication

The most important written communications are: health and safety policy statements; organisation statements identifying health and safety roles and responsibilities; documented performance standards; and supporting organisational and risk control information and procedures. These may be supplemented by mission statements, codes of ethics or statements of philosophy. Extracts from some actual statements of philosophy are shown at Inset 6. These extracts are not intended to act as models but rather to show how such statements can make explicit the values and beliefs which underlie the health and safety policy. An outline of what might be contained in a statement of health and safety policy is given in Inset 7.

AN OUTLINE FOR STATEMENTS OF HEALTH AND SAFETY POLICY

Written statements of health and safety policy should at the very least:

- set the direction for the organisation by communicating senior management's values, beliefs and commitment to health and safety;

- explain the basis of the policy and how it can contribute to business performance (eg by reducing injuries and ill health, protecting the environment and reducing unnecessary losses and liability);

- establish the importance of health and safety objectives in relation to other business objectives;

- commit the organisation to pursuing progressive improvements in health and safety performance, with legal requirements defining the minimum level of achievement;

- explain the responsibilities of managers and the contribution that employees can make to policy implementation outlining the participation procedures;

- commit the organisation to maintaining effective systems of communications on health and safety matters;

- identify the director or key senior manager with overall responsibility for policy formulation, implementation and development;

- commit the leaders of the organisation to supporting the policy with adequate financial and physical resources and by ensuring the competence of all employees and by the provision of any necessary expert advice;

- commit the leaders to planning and regularly reviewing and developing the policy;

- be signed and dated by the director or chief executive of the organisation.

Such written statements of policy will need to be supplemented by statements of organisation and arrangements necessary to implement it.

These documents have to be tailored to the needs of each organisation but generally the degree of detail should be in proportion to the level of complexity and risk: in particular, the greater the risk the more specific instructions need to be. In some cases document control systems may be used to keep track of key documentation. The style of presentation should reflect the needs of the users, whether they be managers, supervisors or other employees of the organisation, or other employers, their employees or self-employed people who share or use the same premises.

In addition to permanent documents, organisations use notices, posters, hand bills, and health and safety newsletters to inform employees about particular issues or about progress in achieving objectives, eg results of inspections, compliance with standards, results of investigations.

The use of notices or posters to support the achievement of specific targets or to improve knowledge of particular risks is more effective than general poster campaigns. Posters can also refer to specific weaknesses which have been identified, for example by accident or incident analysis. The subjects can also be addressed at the same time in 'tool box' talks and other initiatives designed to promote face-to-face discussion and involvement.

Face-to-face discussion

Face-to-face discussion, with an emphasis on the open and honest exchange of views, supports other communication activities by enabling employees to ask questions and make a personal contribution.

Health and safety tours and formal consultative meetings are important opportunities but other systems are used to ensure a good level of communication and participation. These include:
- planned meetings, sometimes known as 'team briefings', at which information is cascaded down the organisation and performance information is given;
- putting health and safety issues on the agenda at all routine management meetings (possibly as the first item);
- monthly or weekly 'tool box talks', or 'tailgate meetings' at which supervisors can discuss health and safety issues with their teams, remind them of critical risks and precautions, and supplement the training effort. These meetings also enable individuals to make their own suggestions about improving safety arrangements.

Flows of information from the organisation

Health and safety information may need to be communicated outside the organisation. For example, it is necessary to supply enforcing agencies with certain accident and ill health data and under Section 6 of the Health and Safety at Work etc Act information must be provided about the safe use of articles and substances supplied for use at work. It may be necessary to communicate with the planning authorities, the emergency services and local residents. On sites where the Control of Industrial Major Accident Hazards (CIMAH) Regulations 1984 apply, these groups must be involved in aspects of emergency planning. In all such cases openness is important and the information given needs to be relevant and to be presented in a form which can be readily understood. Professional advice can be sought on how best to present information so that it can be understood by the audience to whom it is addressed.

Maintaining means of communication in times of emergency is also important and special contingency arrangements may be necessary.

COMPETENCE

Arrangements need to be made to ensure the competence of all employees (including managers) if they are to make the maximum contribution to health and safety. All employees need to be able to work in a safe and healthy manner, and managers need to be aware of relevant legislation and how to manage health and safety effectively. It may also be necessary to examine the abilities of contractors' staff where they work close to, or in collaboration with, direct employees.

Arrangements made by companies who manage health and safety well will include:
- recruitment and placement procedures which ensure that employees (including those at all levels of management), have the necessary physical and mental abilities for their jobs, or can acquire these through training and experience. This may require assessments of individual fitness by medical examination, and tests of physical fitness, or aptitudes and abilities;
- systems to identify health and safety training needs arising from recruitment, changes in staff, plant, substances, technology, processes or working practices; the need to maintain or enhance competence by refresher training; and the presence of contractors' employees, self-employed people or temporary workers;
- systems to provide the information, instruction, training and supporting communications effort needed to meet these needs;
- arrangements to ensure competent cover for staff absences, particularly for staff with critical health and safety responsibilities;
- general health promotion and surveillance schemes which contribute to the maintenance of general health and fitness, and include assessments of fitness for work, rehabilitiation or job adaptation following injury or ill health, however caused.

Training makes an important contribution to the achievement of competence and Inset 8 provides further guidance. Experience of applying skills and knowledge is, however, another important ingredient and needs to be gained under adequate supervision at all levels. Proper supervision helps ensure the development and maintenance of competence and is particularly necessary for those new to a job or undergoing training.

The objective of ensuring the competence of employees is always to maximise their contribution to health and safety either individually or in groups. Working in compliance with performance standards and participating in initiatives such as hazard spotting, problem solving and improving standards all help to develop competence and to contribute to better health and safety performance.

Whatever levels of competence are achieved by managers, supervisors and other employees, professional health and safety advice will sometimes be needed. Advice can be obtained from competent people inside an organisation whose job is to provide health and safety assistance or from outside consultancy organisations. Successful organisations often employ in-house health and safety advisers to co-ordinate the provision of health and safety advice. Their roles and functions are outlined in Inset 9.

TRAINING FOR HEALTH AND SAFETY

Training will help people to acquire the skills, knowledge and attitudes to make them competent in the health and safety aspects of their work - whatever their position in the organisation. It includes formal off-the-job training, instruction to individuals and groups, and on-the-job coaching and counselling. Ensuring that people are competent may demand more than training, for example, a period of supervised experience to practice and develop new skills. Training is therefore only one element in ensuring that people's health and safety performance is satisfactory.

Health and safety requirements should be integrated into job specifications for all employees, and training to meet those requirements calls for a similar approach to that for other business training. A typical training cycle is illustrated here.

Deciding if training is necessary

Training should not be used to compensate either for inadequacies in other aspects of the safety system, such as poorly designed or inadequately protected plant, or for inadequate workstations and procedures which are not designed according to sound ergonomic principles. It may, however, be appropriate to use training as a temporary means of control pending improvements in such areas.

Identifying whether training is necessary demands an understanding of job requirements and the abilities of individuals.

Identifying training needs

Job and task health and safety analyses help to identify health and safety training needs. With new jobs this analysis can involve comparison with similar existing jobs, or possibly by reference to other organisations with similar jobs. With existing jobs the analysis can involve:

• consideration of accident, ill health and incident records relevant to those jobs to identify how such events have occurred and how they can be prevented;

• information from employees about how jobs are done, the sequence of tasks involved and the tools, materials and equipment used;

• observing and questioning employees to understand what they are doing and why. In complex process plant the analysis needs to take account of all the possible consequences of human error, including those which may be remote from the particular task in hand.

With management jobs the analysis should cover both the job itself and the tasks of, and risks run by, subordinates so as to take account of the supervisory part of the job.

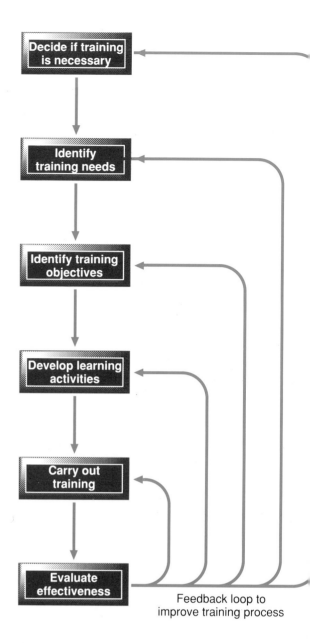

Feedback loop to improve training process

Diagram 5 A typical training cycle

Analysis can be applied to complete jobs or subsidiary tasks. Complete analysis is essential for new starters, but with existing employees the need may be to improve performance on particular tasks.

Job and task health and safety analyses are detailed and resource intensive. They can, however, support the safety management system in a number of respects as well as identifying training needs, including:

• recruitment, selection and placement;

• the identification of critical tasks for which planning and monitoring activities should be a priority;

• the assessment of an individual's performance in a job;

• the assessment of the suitability of an individual for promotion or substitution to a job where health and safety factors are critical.

There are three main types of training needs - organisational, job related and individual.

Organisational needs are common to all those in the organisation. They include knowledge and information about:
- the health and safety policy and the philosophy underlying it;
- the organisational structure and systems for:
- the control of health and safety;
- securing the co-operation of all employees;
- communicating health and safety information;
- ensuring the competence of individuals.

In addition, everyone needs to have an overview of the planning, measuring, reviewing and auditing systems relevant to them and to understand the major risks and how they are controlled.

Job needs are of two main types:
- Management needs which include:
- leadership skills for directors and senior managers responsible for the whole organisation, health and safety advisers, managers and supervisors;
- communication skills;
- techniques of health and safety management;
- training, instruction, coaching and problem solving skills relevant to health and safety;
- understanding of the risks within a manager's area of responsibility, of the health and safety principles which underlie their control and of relevant legislation;
- knowledge of the planning, measuring, reviewing and auditing systems.

For the last aspect, in particular, special consideration should be given to the needs of those who occupy key positions, including those who draw up performance standards: health and safety advisers; those who may have to report on accident, ill health and incident investigations; those involved in review and audit activities; and those who have to implement emergency procedures.

- Non-management needs which include:
- an overview of health and safety principles;
- detailed knowledge of relevant safety performance standards, systems, procedures and rules intended to control the risks of the job, and of the principles underlying them;
- communication and problem solving skills, to encourage effective participation in health and safety activities.

Individual needs are specific to an individual and are generally identified through performance appraisal. They may arise because an individual has not understood formal job training which has been delivered.

Training needs vary over time and regular assessments of needs should be made which cover:
- inducting new starters, including part-time and temporary workers;
- maintaining the performance of established employees (especially in the case of critical emergency procedures) and keeping them up to date with changes;
- changing roles arising from job moves, promotion or the possibility of having to deputise for others;
- introducing new equipment or technology.

Identifying objectives

Having identified all the relevant needs, specific training objectives should be set. Using job and task health and safety analyses, together with an assessment of relative risks, objectives can be prioritised. Once set, objectives can be used as the basis for measuring the effectiveness of training.

Deciding on training methods

Training can be carried out internally or externally. Internal training can involve in-house resources or the use of consultants. A range of equipment and activities may be appropriate depending on the nature of the subject. In general there should be the maximum possible trainee participation.

Carry out training

In some cases training needs may have to be met through closely supervised on-the-job experience. For some high risk jobs and tasks it may be necessary to arrange for such experience to be gained outside the real work situation, for example, at a training facility where simulation exercises can be mounted.

Evaluation and feedback

The effectiveness of training should be measured against the training objectives which have been set. Formal evaluation should be undertaken after training to establish if it has led to the desired improvement in work performance. The results of this evaluation can be used to improve the training process. The effectiveness of training can also be assessed as part of performance measurement activities which aim to identify the underlying causes of substandard performance.

Companies achieving high standards of health and safety give a high priority to health and safety training and develop systematic and documented approaches to it. Resources are allocated according to need and are safeguarded from arbitrary cuts or ▶

▶ modifications such as those arising from cost reduction or rationalisation exercises. This is a reflection of the philosophy which regards people as the organisation's most important resource, and good health and safety performance as contributory to business success.

National and Scottish vocational qualifications

Reference to national vocational qualifications (NVQs) and Scottish vocational qualifications (SVQs) can help with the assessment of health and safety competence. NVQs and SVQs are based on standards developed by lead bodies (LBs) which are made up of representatives of employers, trade unions and professional groups. For each occupational area, LBs identify standards of competence for that occupation and the level of performance required to achieve them. NVQs and SVQs reflect ability to perform activities within an occupation to the standard expected in employment, rather than just the training which has been given.

The competences identified by each LB should include the health and safety competences relevant to that occupational area. However, the standards used relate only to broad areas of competence. In applying the competences it will be necessary to ensure that sufficient detail on relevant health and safety aspects is incorporated into the safety performance standards for the work.

ROLE AND FUNCTIONS OF HEALTH AND SAFETY ADVISERS

Organisations that successfully manage health and safety give health and safety advisers the status and ensure they have the competence to advise management and workers with authority and independence. Subjects on which they advise include:

- health and safety policy formulation and development;
- structuring and operating all parts of the organisation (including the supporting systems) in order to promote a positive health and safety culture and to secure the effective implementation of policy;
- planning for health and safety, including the setting of realistic short and long-term objectives, deciding priorities and establishing adequate performance standards;
- day-to-day implementation and monitoring of policy and plans; including accident and incident investigation, reporting and analysis;
- reviewing performance and auditing the whole safety management system.

To fulfil these functions they have to:

- maintain adequate information systems on relevant law (civil and criminal) and on guidance and developments in general and safety management practice;
- be able to interpret the law and understand how it applies to the organisation;
- establish and keep up-to-date organisational and risk control standards relating to both 'hardware' (such as the place of work and the plant, substances and equipment in use) and 'software' (such as procedures, systems and people) - this task is likely to involve contributions from specialists, for example, architects, engineers, doctors and occupational hygienists;
- establish and maintain procedures for the reporting, investigating and recording and analysis of accidents and incidents;
- establish and maintain adequate and appropriate monitoring and auditing systems;
- present themselves and their advice in an independent and effective manner, safeguarding the confidentiality of personal information such as medical records.

Relationships

Within the organisation

- The position of health and safety advisers in the organisation is such that they support the provision of authoritative and independent advice;
- The post holder has a direct reporting line to directors on matters of policy and authority to stop work which is being carried out in contravention of agreed standards and which puts people at risk of injury.
- Health and safety advisers have responsibility for professional standards and systems and on a large site or in a group of companies may also have line management responsibility for junior health and safety professionals.

Outside the organisation

Health and safety advisers are involved in liaison with a wide range of outside bodies and individuals, including: Local authority environmental health officers and licensing officials; architects and consultants etc; the fire service; contractors; insurance companies; clients and customers; the Health and Safety Executive; the public; equipment suppliers; HM Coroner or Procurator Fiscal; the media; the police; general practitioners; hospital staff.

ORGANISING FOR HEALTH AND SAFETY
SUMMARY

Organisations achieving success in health and safety create and sustain a culture which secures the motivation and involvement of all members of the organisation and the control of risks.

This leads them to establish, operate and maintain structures and systems which aim at:

- securing **control** by:
  - managers who lead by example;
  - clear allocation of responsibilities for policy formulation and development; for planning and reviewing health and safety activities; for the implementation of plans; and for reporting on performance;
  - the allocation of health and safety responsibilities to line managers with specialists acting as advisers;
  - the allocation of health and safety responsibilities to people with the necessary authority and competence who are given the time and resources to carry out their duties effectively;
  - ensuring that individuals are held accountable for their health and safety responsibilities and are motivated by systems of target setting and positive reinforcement;
  - the provision of adequate supervision, instruction and guidance;
  - payment and reward systems which avoid conflict between achieving output targets and health and safety requirements;

- encouraging **co-operation** of employees and safety representatives by:
  - involving them in policy formulation and development and in planning, implementing, measuring, auditing and reviewing performance;
  - making arrangements for involvement at the operational level to supplement more formal participative arrangements;

- securing effective **communication** by means of visible behaviour, written material and face-to-face discussion;

- ensuring **competence** through recruitment, selection, placement, transfer and training and the provision of adequate specialist advice.

FURTHER READING

1 Petersen D *Safety management - a human approach* (2nd edition) 1988 New York Aloray ISBN 0 913690 12 0

2 Findlay JV and Kuhlman RL *Leadership in safety* 1980 Loganville, Georgia Institute Press

3 Petersen D *Human-error reduction and safety management* 1984 New York Aloray ISBN 0 913690 09 0

4 Petersen D *Safe behaviour reinforcement* 1989 New York Aloray ISBN 0 913690 13 9

5 Boydell TH *A guide to job analysis* 1970 British Association for Commercial and Industrial Education ISBN 0 85171 0131

6 Boydell TH *A guide to the identification of training needs* 1976 British Association for Commercial and Industrial Education ISBN 0 85171 059X

7 HSC Advisory Committee on Safety of Nuclear Installations *Study group on human factors - first report on training and related matters* HMSO 1990 ISBN 0 11 885543 3

8 HSC Advisory Committee on Safety of Nuclear Installations *Study group on human factors - second report on human reliability assessment: a critical overview* HMSO 1991 ISBN 0 11 885695 2

9 HSC Advisory Committee on Safety of Nuclear Installations *Study group on human factors - third report on organising for safety* HMSO 1993 ISBN 0 11 882104 0

PLANNING FOR HEALTH AND SAFETY

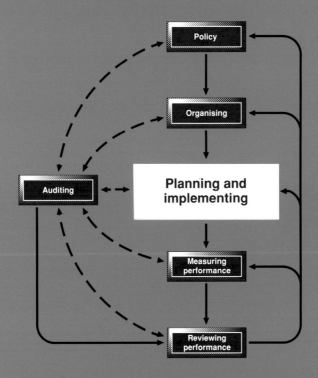

Synopsis

Planning is essential for the effective implementation of health and safety policies. Adequate control can only be achieved by co-ordinated action of all members of the organisation. This chapter examines the planning required to establish and maintain an effective system of health and safety management and, in particular:

- the setting of health and safety objectives; and

- how performance standards are devised and implemented to promote a positive health and safety culture and to control hazards and risks.

PLANNING FOR HEALTH AND SAFETY

The results of successful health and safety management are often expressed as a series of negative outcomes, such as an absence of injuries, ill health, incidents or losses. However, since it is often a matter of chance whether dangerous events cause injury or loss, effective planning is concerned with prevention through the identification, elimination and control of hazards and risks. Moreover, the message from the accident analysis studies referred to in Inset 1 is that effective health and safety planning must cover all situations which have the potential to cause injury, ill health or loss.

The aim of planning for health and safety is to identify the inputs necessary to achieve effective risk control. The process includes:
- identifying objectives which support the aim, and setting targets for their achievement;
- establishing performance standards by which to measure and assess the inputs needed to:
  - develop, maintain and improve an organisational culture which supports the control of risks; and
  - maintain direct control over the risks generated by the activities of the organisation.

Setting objectives

An organisation's immediate health and safety objectives depend on the conditions and standards which currently exist and the first step must be an assessment of these. All organisations, however, need to set objectives for each of the following stages:
1. defining, developing and maintaining the health and safety policy;
2. developing and maintaining organisational arrangements;
3. developing and maintaining performance standards and systems of control.

The balance of activity in each area will be determined by need and, where an organisation is doing little to manage health and safety, the first priority would be on stage 1.

In organisations where health and safety management is more developed, the initial concentration might be more on stages 2 or 3 but in every organisation all three stages must be the subject of regular review. At all stages objectives should be accompanied by specific, measurable, attainable targets including the timescales for their achievement. Personal objectives can then be agreed with individuals to secure the attainment of the general objectives.

In an organisation which is doing little to manage health and safety, the immediate objective would be to review and revise the health and safety policy (within, say, one to three months). This would involve the aspects described in chapter 2 and would include:
- re-defining the corporate commitment to health and safety;
- drafting a new statement of policy;
- establishing new approaches to top level decision making so that health and safety is a factor in all business decisions.

These activities usually take place against a background of a new awareness of the importance of health and safety, health and safety training for managers and often, the injection of outside expertise.

As a new direction on health and safety is established the emphasis should shift to setting objectives of an organisational kind (to be attained within, say, three to six months). Such objectives relate to the issues described in chapter 3 and include:

- establishing or developing the structure, systems and activities for promoting a positive culture, including the role of senior managers;
- assigning responsibilities for key tasks such as planning, the setting of performance standards, measuring performance, and reviewing and auditing;
- establishing or developing the information systems needed for control purposes, such as those for measuring performance, including those for accident, ill health and incident reporting, investigation and analysis;
- identifying the competences needed to implement the policy and specifying the systems that ensure competence at all levels;
- reviewing and developing communications and consultative procedures.

As the new policy and organisational arrangements become established the emphasis shifts to systems of control. Such objectives include:

- training for all employees on the revised policy and the new approach to health and safety management;
- devising performance standards for organisational aspects (such as control, co-operation, competence and communication) and for risk control;
- providing the physical controls needed to meet the requirements of the performance standards ('hardware' controls);
- implementing the new systems and procedures required by the performance standards, together with appropriate training for managers, supervisors and other employees ('software' controls);
- establishing maintenance systems for both the 'hardware' and 'software' controls;
- establishing and developing, measuring, reviewing and auditing systems to monitor the achievement of the performance standards.

Securing these objectives usually requires progress to be made in a number of areas simultaneously. These areas are mutually dependent and the emphasis given to each will change over time. As an organisation develops its health and safety management systems there will be less emphasis on the mechanics of achieving results, as effective monitoring, reviewing and auditing procedures should automatically feed back into improvement and development. The need to maintain the systems, to provide motivation and to promote improvements by setting further objectives will, however, always be present.

As an organisation's health and safety management system becomes more developed, objectives should include raising performance standards above the legal minimum and reducing the number of accidents, ill health and incidents. Successful organisations often also devise performance indicators which act as objectives against which their health and safety performance as a whole can be measured. This is discussed further in chapter 6.

When determining short and long-term objectives (including personal objectives) it is vital that effective consultation takes place involving managers, supervisors and other employees. Everyone involved must believe that the objectives and

Diagram 6 outlines a conceptual framework for identifyi
establish control and measure performance. The diagram
and human resources and information (on the left); work a
the organisation such as products and services, by-pro

Performance standards are required to control the flows of resources and information through the organisation. At the **input stage** (the left hand side of the diagram) the objective is to eliminate and minimise hazards and risks entering the organisation. Here performance standards should cover:

- **physical resources** including:
  - the design, selection, purchase and construction of workplaces;
  - the design, selection, purchase and installation of plant and substances used by the organisation;
  - the plant and substances used by others, such as contractors at work on site;
  - the acquisition of new businesses;

- **human resources** including:
  - the recruitment and selection of all employees;
  - the selection of contracting organisations;

- **information** including:
  - information relating directly to health and safety, such as standards, guidance and aspects of the law;
  - other technical and management information relating to risk control and the development of a positive health and safety culture.

Diagram 6   A framework for setting performance standards
Performance standards are required for each stage of the throughput of resources and information

First stage controls
Control of inputs-
Objective:
　To minimise hazards
　entering the organisation

Physical resources

Human resources

Information

Or

Control

Pr

Commu-
nication

Premises
(the place c
work)

Second stage controls
Control of work activities-
Objectives:
　To eliminate and minimise risks inside the orga
　To create a supportive organisational culture

At the **internal activity stage** (the middle part of the diagram), risks are created where people interact with their jobs - signified by the red area in the diagram - and the objective is to eliminate or minimise risks arising inside the organisation. Here performance standards should cover:

- the four elements involved in creating a positive health and safety culture:
control, **communication**, **co-operation** and **competence**;

- the four elements concerned with work activities and risk creation namely:
premises - including the place of work, entrances and exits, the general working environment, welfare facilities, and all plant and facilities which are part of the fixed structure,

such as permanent electrical installations;
plant and substances - including the arrangements for their handling, transport, storage and use;
procedures - including the design of jobs and wo procedures and all aspects of the way the work is done;
people - including the placement of employees, their competence for the job and any health surveillance which may be required.

When specifying internal activity performance standards is necessary in each case to consider:

- the operation of the production system in the 'steady state', including routine and non-routine activities;
- the production system in the 'steady state' during

ERFORMANCE STANDARDS

areas for which performance standards are necessary to
s three stages: inputs to the organisation such as physical
es within the organisation (in the middle); and outputs from
and information (on the right).

At the **output stage** (the right hand side of the diagram) the objective is to minimise the risks to people outside the organisation whether from work activities themselves or from the products or services supplied. Here performance standards should cover:

- products and services, and include consideration of:
  - design and research on the health and safety and safe use of products and services, including surveillance of users to identify evidence of harm;
  - the delivery and transport of products including packaging, labelling and intermediate storage;
  - the installation, setting up, cleaning and maintenance of products undertaken by either employees or contractors;

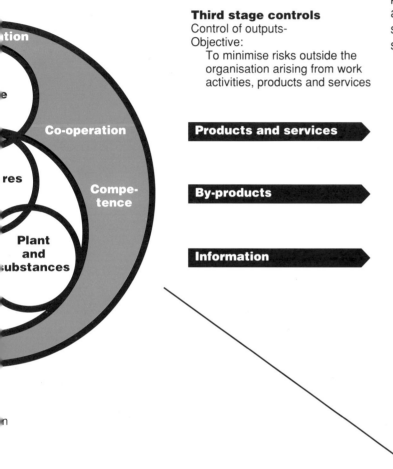

Third stage controls
Control of outputs-
Objective:
    To minimise risks outside the
    organisation arising from work
    activities, products and services

Products and services

By-products

Information

- by-products of the work activities, such as:
  - offsite risks which might arise from the organisation's work activities both at fixed or transient sites;
  - outputs to the environment - particularly wastes and atmospheric emissions;
  - the disposal of plant, equipment and substances (including wastes);

- information, for example:
  - the health and safety information provided to those transporting, handling, storing, purchasing, using or disposing of products;
  - the information provided to those who may be affected by work activities, such as members of the public, other employers and their employees, the emergency services and planning authorities.

maintenance, including the maintenance activity itself, whether undertaken by contractors or on-site staff;
- planned changes from the 'steady state', arising from any change in premises, plant, substances, procedures, people or information;
- foreseeable emergencies giving rise to serious and imminent danger, such as fire, injuries, ill health, incidents or the failure of control equipment (including first aid, emergency planning and procedures for the management of emergencies, and identification and control of danger areas);
- decommissioning, dismantling and removal of facilities, plant, equipment or substances.

Appendix 3 provides further guidance on setting performance standards by outlining the minimum objectives for performance standards in each of the areas outlined here.

timescales are realistic for commitment and 'ownership' to be secured.

Decisions about priorities and the allocation of resources should reflect the fact that the ultimate aim is to minimise risks within the organisation while the immediate objective may be to achieve a level of performance which complies with the relevant legal requirements. The timescales for improvements should reflect the levels of risk involved and the costs of the remedial measures. Where fundamental changes cannot be made right away or within a reasonable time, short-term measures should be taken to minimise the risks in the meantime. The process of assessing risks is discussed later in this chapter.

SETTING PERFORMANCE STANDARDS

Performance standards need to be established progressively after a thorough analysis of the needs of the organisation and of existing, and possible future, risks. Performance standards should cover both organisational procedures and the control of specific risks.

Inset 10 provides a framework for identifying the main areas for which performance standards are needed. Appendix 3 provides further guidance on setting performance standards by outlining minimum objectives for the standards necessary in each area.

Organisational performance standards
The objectives of organisational performance standards are to ensure:
- the consistent implementation of plans and performance standards;
- the effective communication of the corporate belief in the importance of health and safety and the creation of a positive health and safety culture;
- improved understanding and control of risks.

Control
Performance standards for control are intended to secure the effective operation of the management system and continued improvement in risk control through the development and maintenance of a positive culture. They should therefore establish the nature and frequency of, for example:
- policy formulation and development;
- organisational development;
- planning, measuring and reviewing organisational and individual performance;
- auditing the whole health and safety management system.

Co-operation
In this area, performance standards should establish the nature and frequency of, for example:
- health and safety committee meetings and similar formal consultative meetings;
- the preparation of the minutes of health and safety committees and similar meetings together with action points;
- problem solving meetings or 'safety circle meetings'.

Communication

Performance standards for communication should establish the nature and frequency of, for example:

- the collection of information from external sources;
- senior management involvement in formal consultative arrangements, safety tours, etc;
- senior and other management involvement in accident, ill health and incident investigation;
- the involvement of senior and other management in planning, monitoring, auditing and reviewing performance;
- discussion of health and safety matters at management meetings;
- systems for cascading information;
- 'tool-box' talks;
- documentation of policy statements, organisation statements, performance standards, rules and procedures;
- use of posters, bulletins, newspapers and other similar means of communication;
- the preparation and dissemination of information to outside organisations and individuals.

Competence

Performance standards for arrangements to secure the competence of employees should, amongst other things, cover:

- recruitment and placement procedures;
- the provision of information and training;
- arrangements for supervised on-the-job experience;
- the availability of competent cover for staff absences;
- general health promotion and surveillance.

Performance standards for the control of hazards and risks

Performance standards are necessary to control the risks arising from activities, products and services, and are required for at least those areas outlined in Inset 10. They are necessary to control the complete cycle of activities ranging from the selection of resources and information, the design and operation of working systems, the design and delivery of product and services, and the control and disposal of waste. The control of risks is necessary to secure compliance with the requirements of the Health and Safety at Work etc Act 1974 and the relevant statutory provisions made under that Act and earlier legislation.

Setting performance standards involves four stages:
- **hazard identification** - identifying hazards which are the potential causes of harm;
- **risk assessment** - assessing the risk which may arise from hazards;
- **risk control** - deciding on suitable measures to eliminate or control risk;
- **implementing and maintaining control measures** - implementing standards and ensuring that they are effective.

These four stages form the fundamental principles of occupational health and safety and of making decisions about the control of risks. This approach is applicable both to the control of health risks and safety risks. (Health risks do however present distinctive features which require a particular approach - Inset 11 provides further details.) These principles are now increasingly incorporated into legislation which aims to improve the management of health and safety, eg The Management of

CONTROLLING HEALTH RISKS

The principles of controlling both safety and health risks are the same.

The application of the principles to health risks requires a particular approach because of the inherent features of the risk.

The distinctive features of health risks include:
- Ill health which often results not from immediate injury but from complex biological processes such as the repair of repeated damage (irritant dermatitis), immune responses (asthma), or abnormal cell behaviour (cancers). There is individual variation in response.
- These processes may take place over a long period (eg asbestos related diseases). Hence hazards may only become apparent after many people have been put at risk. Cases of disease may continue for decades after exposure has been controlled.
- The same disease may have both occupational and non-occupational causes (eg, asthma, back pain, lung cancer). The link with occupation can sometimes be established in an individual but confirmation of an occupational cause usually comes from studies comparing frequency of disease in exposed and non-exposed groups.
- Exposure to disease risks is not always apparent. Measurement of risk factors is often required. The probability of disease occurring often depends on the level of exposure over a long period. The severity of many diseases, but not all (eg, cancers) also depends on the level of exposure.

Implications for successful health risk control:
- The complexity of many health risks means that the identification of health hazards and health risk assessments will generally require greater input of appropriate in-house or external consultant expertise than that required for many safety assessments.
- The assessment of health risks often requires the measurement of exposure, calling for specific monitoring and assessment techniques and the competence to use them.
- While health risks arising from the use of substances can be controlled by physical control measures, systems of work and personal protective equipment, the operation of which can be measured, confirmation of the adequacy of control will often require measurements of the working environment to check that exposures are within pre-set limits. Sometimes surveillance of those at risk to detect excessive uptake of a substance (biological monitoring) or early signs of harm (health surveillance), may also be necessary. These techniques require occupational hygiene and clinical skills and those at risk expect that individual results will need to be handled within a framework of medical confidentiality.

Health and Safety at Work Regulations 1992 (MHSW), and the Control of Substances Hazardous to Health Regulations 1988 (COSHH).

In practice many decisions in these four areas are taken as a whole, eg where the identification stage reveals a well known hazard which involves a known risk and demands well tried and tested methods of control and consequent maintenance. For example, stairs present an established risk of slipping, tripping and falling and require traditional methods of control such as good construction, the use of hand rails and the provision of non-slip surfaces along with the need to keep stairs free of obstructions. In other more complex situations decisions are necessary at each stage and the nature of these are outlined below.

Hazard Identification

Seeking out and identifying hazards is an essential first step in risk control. Adequate information is necessary and reference should be made to relevant sources such as:
- legislation and supporting approved codes of practice which give practical guidance and include basic minimum requirements;
- Health and Safety Executive guidance;

- product information provided under Section 6 of the Health and Safety at Work etc Act 1974;
- relevant British and international standards;
- industry or trade association guidance;
- the personal knowledge and experience of managers and employees;
- accident, ill health and incident data from within the organisation, from other organisations or from central sources;
- expert advice and opinion.

The identification of hazards should involve a critical appraisal of all activities to take account of hazards to employees, others affected by activities (eg, members of the public and contractors) and to those using products and services. Adequate hazard identification requires a complete understanding of the working situation. Employee and safety representative participation can make a useful contribution to this process.

In the simplest cases hazards can be identified by observation, comparing the circumstances with the relevant information. For example, single storey premises will not present the hazards associated with stairs. In more complex cases measurements such as air sampling or examining the methods of machine operation may be necessary to identify the presence of hazards presented by chemicals or machinery. In the most complex or high risk cases (for example, in the chemical or nuclear industry) special techniques and systems may be required such as hazard and operability studies (HAZOPS) and hazard analysis systems such as event or fault tree analysis. Specialist advice may be necessary in choosing and applying the most appropriate techniques.

Risk assessment

Assessing risks is a general requirement of the MHSW Regulations 1992. Assessing risks is necessary in order to identify their relative importance and to obtain information about their extent and nature. This will help in deciding on methods of control. Knowledge of both areas is necessary in order to identify where to place the major effort in prevention and control, and in order to make decisions on the adequacy of control measures.

Determining the relative importance of risks involves deciding on the severity of the hazard and the likelihood of occurrence. There is no general formula for rating risks in relative importance but a number of techniques have been developed to assist in decision making and these are described in Inset 12. As a general guide the emphasis should be given to risks which present the greatest severity. Risks which could create catastrophic consequences, albeit infrequently, should be given greater priority than those risks which create only small losses. The likelihood of occurrence (expressed as a frequency or a probability) however, cannot be ignored eg, where two risks have the same severity the one most likely to occur should take precedence.

Assessing risks to help determine control measures can be undertaken qualitatively or quantitatively. In the simplest case risks may be assessed by reference to clear cut legal limits, for example, people are liable to fall a distance of two metres from an open edge or they are not. In more complex situations qualitative judgements may be necessary within a framework set by legal standards and guidance. The Control of Substances Hazardous to Health Regulations 1988 (COSHH) and the accompanying approved codes of practice establish a decision making framework where hazardous substances are used. British Standard 5304:1988,

ASSESSING THE RELATIVE IMPORTANCE OF HEALTH AND SAFETY RISKS

Determining the relative importance of risks is an important element in risk assessment so as to identify high risk areas which will demand a greater proportion of resources, both in the level of risk control, and in the level of maintenance control measures. Rating or ranking risks in relative importance can contribute to establishing risk control priorities.

While there is no general formula for rating risks a number of techniques have been developed to assist in decision making. These should be distinguished from the detailed risk assessments needed to establish the levels of risk control to satisfy legal standards. They involve only a means of ranking hazards and risks. Some systems rank hazards, others rank risks. Assessing relative risk involves some means of estimating the likelihood of occurrence and the severity of a hazard. A simple form of risk estimation is described below to illustrate the general principles.

Simple risk estimation

Hazards - the potential to cause harm will vary in severity. The effect of a hazard may, for example be rated:

3 - MAJOR
*for example, death or major injury
(as defined in RIDDOR);*
2 - SERIOUS
*for example, injuries where people may be off work for
more than three days;*
1 - SLIGHT
*for example, all other injuries including those where
people are off for periods of up to three days.*

Harm may not arise from exposure to a hazard in every case and in practice the likelihood of harm will be affected by the organisation of the work, how effectively the hazard is controlled and, the extent and nature of exposure to it. In the case of health risks the latent effects and the susceptibility of individuals will also be relevent. Judgements about likelihood will also be affected by experience of working with a hazard, for example the analysis of accident, ill health and incident data may provide a clue. The likelihood of harm may be rated:

3 - HIGH
where it is certain or near certain that harm will occur;
2 - MEDIUM
where harm will occur frequently;
1 - LOW
where harm will seldom occur.

In this case risk can be defined as the combination of the severity of the hazard with the likelihood of its occurrence, or:

RISK = HAZARD SEVERITY x LIKELIHOOD OF OCCURRENCE

By multiplying together those numbers which represent the severity of a hazard and the likelihood of occurrence, a single figure is obtained which allows risks to be compared. Where hazards affect more than one person the resulting multiple could perhaps be multiplied by the number of people exposed to obtain a better comparison.

This example presents the most simplified method of estimating relative risk. In practice organisations need to devise systems suited to their own needs. Hazard rating systems have been developed by Dow (reference 1) and ICI (the Mond Index - reference 2). Simplified relative risk assessment systems have been developed by amongst others Rowe (reference 3), by the International Loss Control Institute (reference 4) and by other independent consultants (reference 5).

Systems of assessing relative risk can contribute not only to establishing risk control priorities but also assist in prioritising other activities. Questions of importance and urgency arise at several other stages in the implementation of a preventive health and safety policy, for example:
- when deciding health and safety objectives;
- when identifying high risk areas which require more detailed maintenance and monitoring;
- when deciding priorities for training and improving levels of competence;
- when deciding what, if any, immediate action is necessary to prevent further injury following an accident;
- when deciding what, if any, immediate action is necessary to prevent injury following an incident or the discovery of a hazard;
- when reviewing the results of monitoring activities and the results of injury, ill health and incident investigations;
- when deciding the extent of the resources required and the speed of the response which should be made following a particular accident or incident.

Code of practice for safety of machinery, establishes a framework for decisions about machinery guarding. Quantitative risk assessment (QRA) techniques may be used as a basis for making decisions in more complex industries. Specific reference to the use of QRA is contained in the Offshore Installations (Safety Case) Regulations 1992 (Safety Case Regulations).

Assessing risks will demand a thorough knowledge of all activities and working practices and again the knowledge of the employees and safety representatives involved will prove valuable. Risk assessments should be carried out by competent people, and professional health and safety advice may be necessary in some cases, especially in the choice of appropriate QRA techniques and the interpretation of results.

Risk control

When risks have been analysed and assessed decisions can be made about control measures.

All final decisions about risk control measures must take into account the relevant legal requirements which establish minimum levels of risk prevention or control. Some of the duties imposed by the Health and Safety at Work etc Act 1974 and the relevant statutory provisions are absolute and must be complied with, for example, the requirements within the Factories Act 1961 which prescribes that all dangerous machinery should be adequately guarded. Many requirements are, however, qualified by the words, 'so far as is reasonably practicable', or 'so far as is practicable'. Other duties require the use of 'best practicable means' - often used in the context of controlling sources of environmental pollution such as emissions to the atmosphere. Further guidance on the meaning of these three expressions is provided in Inset 13.

Where legal requirements demand an assessment of cost, information about the relative costs, effectiveness and reliability of different control measures will be necessary so that decisions about acceptable levels of control can be made.

Decisions about the reliability of controls can be guided by reference to the preferred hierarchy of control which has now been incorporated into new regulations such as MHSW and COSHH. The following is a summary of the preferred hierarchy of risk control principles:

1. Eliminate risks by substituting the dangerous by the less dangerous, eg:
   - by using a less hazardous substance;
   - by substituting a type of machine which is better guarded to achieve the same product;
   - by avoiding the use of certain processes, eg by buying from subcontractors;

2. Combating risks at source by engineering controls and giving collective protective measures priority, eg:
   - separating the operator from the risk of exposure to a known hazardous substance by enclosing the process;
   - by protecting the dangerous parts of a machine by guarding;
   - designing process machinery and work activities to minimise the release, suppress or contain air borne hazards;
   - by designing machinery which is remotely operated and to which materials are fed automatically thus separating the operator from danger areas.

'SO FAR AS IS REASONABLY PRACTICABLE',
'SO FAR AS IS PRACTICABLE',
and 'BEST PRACTICABLE MEANS'

Although none of these expressions are defined in the Health and Safety at Work etc Act 1974, they have acquired meanings through many interpretations by the courts and it is the courts which, in the final analysis, decide their application in particular cases.

To carry out a duty **so far as is reasonably practicable** means that the degree of risk in a particular activity or environment can be balanced against the time, trouble, cost and physical difficulty of taking measures to avoid the risk. If these are so disproportionate to the risk that it would be unreasonable for the persons concerned to have to incur them to prevent it, they are not obliged to do so. The greater the risk, the more likely it is that it is reasonable to go to very substantial expense, trouble and invention to reduce it. But if the consequences and the extent of a risk are small, insistence on great expense would not be considered reasonable. It is important to remember that the judgement is an objective one and the size or financial position of the employer are immaterial.

So far as is practicable, without the qualifying word 'reasonably', implies a stricter standard. This term generally embraces whatever is technically possible in the light of current knowledge, which the person concerned had or ought to have had at the time. The cost, time and trouble involved are not to be taken into account.

The meaning of **best practicable means** can vary depending on its context and ultimately it is for the courts to decide. Where the law prescribes that 'best practicable means' should be employed, it is usual for the regulating authority to indicate its view of what is practicable in notes or even agreements with particular firms or industries. Both these notes or agreements and the views likely to be taken by a court will be influenced by considerations of cost and technical practicability. But the view generally adopted by HSE inspectors is that an element of reasonableness is involved in considering whether the best practicable means had been used in a particular situation.

3 Minimising risk by the design of suitable systems of working.

4 Minimising risk by the use of personal protective clothing and equipment, which should only be used as a last resort.

The hierarchy reflects that risk elimination and risk control by the use of physical engineering controls and safeguards can be more reliably maintained than those which rely solely on people.

Where a range of control measures are available, it will be necessary to weigh up the relative costs of each against the degree of control each provides, both in the short and long term. Some control measures, such as eliminating a risk by choosing a safer alternative substance or machine, provide a high degree of control and are reliable. Physical safeguards such as guarding a machine or enclosing a hazardous process need to be maintained. In making decisions about risk control, it will therefore be necessary to consider the degree of control and the reliability of the control measures along with the costs of both providing **and** maintaining the measure.

The design of all control measures should take account of the human factors aspects which were outlined in Inset 2. In successful organisations the design of risk controls is fully integrated into plant and work design procedures so that specifications simultaneously satisfy output, quality, and health and safety requirements.

Implementing and maintaining risk control measures

The practical implementation of control measures is assisted by their good design. The full implementation of adequate control measures may take time, and at each stage where full controls cannot be achieved, adequate steps should be taken in the interim to minimise the risks. The techniques for assessing relative risks outlined in Inset 12 can be used to identify the most important risks which should be dealt with first.

Control measures should be recorded as a means of ensuring their consistent implementation. Recording assessments and control measures is a specific requirement under some sets of regulations including MHSW, COSHH, the Control of Industrial Major Accident Hazards Regulations 1984 (CIMAH) and the Safety Case Regulations. The MHSW Regulations require that an employer with five or more employees should record the significant findings of each assessment and any group of their employees identified by it as being especially at risk. The COSHH Regulations require that the evaluation of risk, the specification and implementation of control measures and the date of further reviews should be recorded. Under the CIMAH Regulations a safety report is required which documents, amongst other specific things, the description of the hazards presented by the dangerous substances on site, a description of the potential sources of major accidents and a description of the measures to prevent, control or minimise the consequences of any major accident. The Safety Case Regulations contain similar requirements in respect of safety cases prepared for offshore installations.

Performance standards for risk control should be documented to a level of detail which reflects the degree of risk. The control of relatively minor risks affecting all employees, such as ensuring free passageways and gangways, can be dealt with by a number of simply stated general rules. The control of more specific risks may require specific standards and control procedures. The control of high risk activities may require detailed performance standards and procedures which need to be strictly followed, for example, a permit-to-work system which ensures close supervision during implementation.

Maintaining risk control measures requires adequate inspection, maintenance and monitoring procedures to secure continued operation. This will include review procedures to examine risk assessment and control measures in the light of changes and technological developments. The type of maintenance, its frequency and depth will reflect the extent and nature of the risk revealed by the risk assessment process. The balance of resources devoted to the various control measures will also reflect the relative importance of the risks.

Part of the maintenance and monitoring arrangements will include ensuring that people comply with health and safety procedures. Even where risk control measures are well developed and take full account of human limitations and fallibilities, there remains the challenge of ensuring that they are complied with consistently. The main way of achieving this is by means of measuring and rewarding the extent of compliance according to the maxim, "what gets rewarded gets done".

Some organisations have applied performance management techniques to strengthen their health and safety system. Others have sought to motivate employees by using behaviour modification techniques designed to promote and reward safe behaviour and reduce unsafe behaviour. Behaviour modification techniques are now being recognised by successful companies as important techniques in motivating and sustaining positive behaviour, and in promoting consistently good safety performance. Chapter 5 examines in more detail the whole area of measuring health and safety performance.

PLANNING FOR HEALTH AND SAFETY
SUMMARY

Organisations achieving success in health and safety minimise risks in their operation by drawing up plans and setting performance standards with the aim of eliminating and controlling risks. They establish, operate and maintain planning systems which:

- identify objectives and targets for their achievement within a specific period;

- set performance standards for management actions designed to initiate, develop, maintain and improve a positive health and safety culture in the four key areas - control, competence, communication and co-operation;

- set performance standards for the control of risks which are based on hazard identification and risk assessment, which take legal requirements as the minimum acceptable standard of performance and which emphasise:

  - the elimination of risks by the substitution of safer premises, plant or substances and, where this is not reasonably practicable,

  - the control of risks by physical safeguards which minimise the need for employees to follow detailed systems of work or to use protective equipment;

- establish priorities for the provision and maintenance of control measures by the use of risk assessment techniques, giving priority to high risk areas and adopting temporary control measures to minimise risks where satisfactory control cannot be achieved immediately;

- set performance standards for the control of risks both to employees and to others who may be affected by the organisation's activities, products and services;

- ensure the adequate documentation of all performance standards - the detail of documentation reflecting the degree of risk.

FURTHER READING

1 American Institute of Chemical Engineers *Fire and explosion index hazard classification guide* 6th ed New York 1987 ISBN 0 81690 438 3

2 ICI plc *The Mond index: (How to identify, assess and minimise potential hazards on chemical plant units for new and existing processes)* 2nd ed 1985
Ref No IC 07707 Available from ICI Report Centre Research and Technology Department, Runcorn Heath PO Box 13 Tel: 0928 513309

3 Rowe G Setting safety priorities: A technical and social process *Journal of Occupational Accidents* 1990 Vol 12 31-40

4 Bird Jnr FE and Germain GL *Practical loss control leadership* (chapters 6 & 7) International Loss Control Institute 1986 ISBN 0 88061 054 9

5 Steel C Risk estimation *Safety Practitioner* June 1990 Vol 8 No 6 20-21

6 HSE *Quantified risk assessment: Its input to decision making* 1989 HMSO ISBN 0 11 885499 2

7 HSE *COSHH assessments: A step-by-step guide to assessment and the skills needed for it* 1988 HMSO ISBN 0 11 885470 4

8 Krause TR, Hidley JH, Hodson SJ *The behaviour-based safety process: Managing involvement for an injury free culture* Van Nostrand Reinhold 1990 ISBN 0 442 00227 0

9 Sulzer-Azaroff B The modification of occupational safety behaviour *Journal of Occupational Accidents* Nov 1987 Vol 9 No 3 177-197

10 Sheffield Training Agency *Performance management: The Cambridgeshire experience* Investing in People II - Management Development Series Deloitt, Hoskins and Sells Ref: ATL 121 PP51/8349/690/24

11 The Institution of Chemical Engineers Rugby *Loss prevention: Practical risk assessment: students workbook* 1989 ISBN 0 852 95245 7

12 HSC *Management of health and safety at work* Approved Code of Practice 1992 HMSO ISBN 0 11 886330 4

13 HSE *A guide to the Offshore Installations (Safety Case) Regulations 1992* 1992 HMSO, ISBN 0 11 882055 9

14 HSE *Work equipment* Guidance on Regulations 1992 HMSO ISBN 0 11 886332 0

15 HSE *Manual handling* Guidance on Regulations 1992 HMSO ISBN 0 11 886335 5

16 HSC *Workplace health, safety and welfare* Approved Code of Practice 1992 HMSO ISBN 0 11 886333 9

17 HSE *Personal protective equipment at work* Guidance on Regulations 1992 HMSO, ISBN 0 11 886334 7

18 HSE *Display screen equipment work* Guidance on Regulations 1992 HMSO ISBN 0 11 886331 2

MEASURING PERFORMANCE

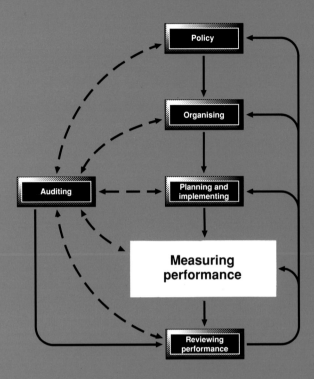

Synopsis

Measurement is an essential aspect of maintaining and improving health and safety performance. This chapter describes the features of:

- active systems which monitor the achievement of plans and the extent of compliance with standards; and

- reactive systems which monitor accidents, ill health and incidents.

Both systems generate information on levels of performance and effective systems of reporting, investigating, recording and analysing data are necessary to support them. The purpose and design of such systems is also examined.

MEASURING PERFORMANCE

A low accident rate, even over a period of years, is no guarantee that risks are being effectively controlled and will not lead to injuries, ill health or loss in the future. This is particularly so in organisations where there is a low probability of accidents but where major hazards are present. In such cases the historical incidence of reported accidents can be an unreliable, deceptive indicator of safety performance. In order to ensure that an organisation's policy is effectively implemented, the steps taken to develop a positive health and safety culture and to control risks need to be measured.

Organisations achieving success in health and safety measure performance against predetermined plans and standards, assessing their implementation and effectiveness in order to identify the need for remedial action. Monitoring activities also signal management commitment to health and safety objectives in general and are an essential part of developing a positive health and safety culture. Like planning, monitoring should be a line management responsibility and the arrangements should cover the whole range of health and safety performance standards which have been established. Two types of system are needed:
- active systems which monitor the achievement of objectives and the extent of compliance with standards; and
- reactive systems which monitor accidents, ill health, incidents and other evidence of deficient health and safety performance, such as hazard reports.

Both types of monitoring system need to be supported by procedures which ensure adequate investigation of the causes of substandard performance.

ACTIVE MONITORING SYSTEMS

Active monitoring provides essential feedback on performance before an accident, ill health or an incident. It involves checking compliance with performance standards and the achievement of specific objectives. Its primary purpose is to measure success and reinforce positive achievement by rewarding good work, not to penalise failure.

INSPECTION

A system for the inspection of plant and facilities forms an essential part of any active monitoring programme. It includes inspections and examinations which form part of arrangements for the preventive maintenance of plant and equipment. Many of these are legal requirements, including, for example: the thorough examination and inspection of pressure vessels, lifts, cranes, chains, ropes, lifting tackle, scaffolds, and supports for the sides of trenches; the thorough examination and test of local exhaust ventilation and air sampling to check its efficiency.

The inspection programme should, however, be more comprehensive than that, covering all areas and all relevant performance standards, and taking account of the risks involved in the work. Low risks can be dealt with by means of general inspections of large areas and covering a wide range of issues, such as the general condition of premises, floors, passages, stairs, lighting, welfare facilities, and first-aid facilities. Inspections of this type might take place every month or two. High risks require more frequent and detailed inspections and closer examination, for example by means of weekly inspections of high risk plant and important control equipment. In extreme cases, daily or pre-use inspections and checks may be required as, for example, with pre-use checks on mobile plant.

Schedules should be drawn up specifying the frequency of inspections to satisfy specific legal requirements and to reflect risk priorities. These should be supplemented by inspection forms and check lists to ensure consistency and to provide records for follow-up action and further evaluation and analysis.

Managers should be given the responsibility for monitoring the achievement of those objectives and measuring compliance with those standards for which they and their subordinates are responsible. Successive levels of monitoring should reflect the structure of the organisation. Managers responsible for the direct implementation of standards should monitor compliance in detail. Above this immediate level of control monitoring can take the form of reports which demonstrate whether adequate first line monitoring is taking place. Such reports should be supplemented by an examination of a sample of monitoring activities to check the quality of the work.

The various forms and levels of active monitoring include:

- indirect monitoring of performance standards where managers check the quantity and quality of monitoring activities undertaken by their subordinates;
- procedures to monitor the achievement of objectives allocated to managers or sections by means, for example, of monthly or quarterly reports or returns;
- the periodic examination of documents to check that standards relating to the promotion of the safety culture are complied with, for example, that suitable objectives have been established for each manager; that these are regularly reviewed; that all training needs have been assessed and recorded; and that these training needs are being met;
- the systematic inspection of premises, plant and equipment by supervisors, maintenance staff or a joint team of management, safety representatives and other employees, to ensure the continued effective operation of hardware controls. Inset 14 provides further guidance on this aspect;
- environmental monitoring and health surveillance to check on the effectiveness of health control measures and detect early signs of harm to health;
- systematic direct observation of work and behaviour by first line supervisors to assess compliance with procedures, rules and systems - particularly when directly concerned with risk control;

Inspections must be undertaken by people who are competent to identify the relevant hazards and risks and to assess the conditions found. Full records should be kept of each inspection with details of both positive and negative findings.

When shortcomings are found the decision processes illustrated in Diagram 7 should be followed. These involve identifying any instances were immediate action is necessary; undertaking sufficient investigation to identify both the immediate and the underlying causes of the shortcomings; analysing and reviewing findings; planning remedial action; and setting such action in progress.

The design of inspection forms can help in planning and initiating remedial action by requiring those responsible for inspection to mark or rank deficiencies according to their relative importance. A list summarising remedial action can also be used as the basis for a tracking system to check on implementation. Inspection forms should be analysed periodically to identify if there are any common features or trends which reveal underlying weaknesses in the health and safety management system.

As an organisation's understanding of its risks and their control develops, the frequency and depth of inspection may be changed to improve the monitoring process. This may involve the redesign of inspection regimes, inspection forms and check lists.

- the operation of audit systems, as described in the next chapter;
- consideration of regular reports on health and safety performance at main board level.

Monitoring effort should reflect the extent of the risks involved. Monitoring activities should be concentrated in areas where they produce the most benefit and lead to the greatest control of risks, so that high risk premises, plant, procedures and tasks are monitored in more detail and/or more frequently. For example, in a workshop with 50 procedures each containing one high risk task or element, it might be appropriate to monitor compliance by checking one procedure each week, thus covering all procedures within a year. The high risk elements might, however, need to be checked more frequently, say four times a year at a rate of four per week. A system would need to be established to ensure that these frequencies were being met.

Regular monitoring can sometimes usefully be supplemented by:
- random observation, including observation by senior managers on 'health and safety tours';
- questionnaire surveys of managers and other employees (possibly on an anonymous basis) to assess behaviour and attitudes towards health and safety;
- inspections by safety representatives or other employee representatives.

Active monitoring should provide the basis for decision making about improvements as well as providing a basis for rewarding good health and safety performance. Such reinforcement increases motivation to achieve continued improvements in performance.

REACTIVE MONITORING SYSTEMS

Reactive systems monitor accidents, ill health and incidents. They require the recognition and reporting of:
- injuries and cases of ill health;
- other loss events, eg damage to property;
- incidents (including all those which had the potential to cause injury, ill health or loss);
- hazards;
- weaknesses or omissions in performance standards.

Securing the reporting of serious injuries and ill health generally presents few problems for most organisations. However, the reporting of minor injuries, other loss events, incidents, and hazards may prove more difficult. In successful organisations the reporting of all events is promoted by:
- training which clarifies the underlying objectives and reasons for identifying all relevant events;
- a culture which emphasises an observant and responsive approach and the critical importance of improving systems of control before harm occurs, and which encourages open, honest communication;
- cross referencing and checking first-aid treatments, health records, maintenance reports, fire reports and insurance claims, to identify any otherwise unreported events.

INVESTIGATION AND RESPONSE SYSTEMS FOR ACTIVE AND REACTIVE MONITORING

Systems are needed to ensure a consistent response to, and thorough investigation of, substandard performance. The results of investigations also need to be analysed and reviewed so as to identify common features and trends which might reveal areas for general improvement. These systems must be operated by staff with the necessary level of competence.

A common series of steps can be identified for responding to both active and reactive monitoring. These are summarised in Diagram 7 and are described overleaf.

Diagram 7

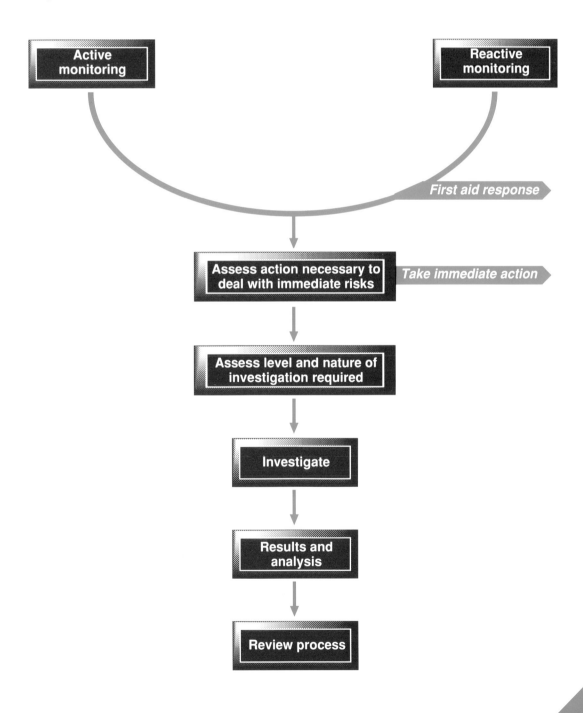

Actions necessary to deal with immediate risks

Information from both active and reactive monitoring systems must be evaluated promptly to identify immediate risks and to ensure that appropriate remedial action is taken without delay. The identification of such situations may require the use of a formal but simplified risk estimation technique (see Inset 12). Where there is a risk of a major incident the appropriate response would be the implementation of established emergency procedures or disaster management plans.

Level and nature of investigation

The level and nature of investigations should reflect the significance of the event being investigated. The greatest effort should be concentrated on those involving significant injuries, ill health or loss **and** on those which had the potential to cause widespread or serious injury or loss. Investigations should be designed to identify reasons for substandard performance, to identify underlying failures in health and safety management systems, to learn from events, and to prevent recurrences. Investigations are also necessary to:

- satisfy legal recording and reporting requirements;
- collect information which may be needed if the incident becomes the subject of legal action;
- collect information for potential insurance claims;
- maintain records for other purposes specific to the organisation.

Most investigations are carried out by line managers with health and safety advisers and technical staff acting in a supporting role, where necessary. Progressively more senior levels of management should be involved in investigating events involving more serious actual or potential consequences. In most serious cases investigation teams or boards, consisting of managers, specialists and employee representatives may be employed.

The form of investigation

Investigations should identify both the immediate circumstances and the underlying organisational causes. Recommendations should be made on measures to improve the management systems and performance standards.

KEY DATA TO BE COVERED IN ACCIDENT, ILL HEALTH AND INCIDENT REPORTS

The event

- Details of any injured employee(s), including age, sex, experience, training etc;

- A description of the circumstances, including the place, time of day and conditions;

- Details of the event, including:
  - any actions which led directly to the event;
  - the direct causes of any injuries, ill health or other loss;
  - the immediate causes of the event;
  - the underlying causes - for example, failures in systems of control; failures of management or supervision; lack of competence; inadequate training; inadequate performance standards; or failure to address human factor issues;

- Details of the outcomes including in particular:
  - the nature of the outcome - for example, injuries, or ill health to employees or members of the public; damage to property; process disruptions; emissions to the environment; creation of hazards;
  - the severity of the harm caused including injuries, ill health and losses;
  - the immediate management response to the

Investigation techniques should ensure that the whole circumstances are considered including human factors' issues and including:

- organisational aspects and systems, including relevant policies, standards, rules and procedures;
- the job, including the premises, plant, substances and procedures in use and their effect on the employee(s) concerned;
- the employee(s) including their behaviour, suitability and competence - along with the reasons for any deficiency in performance.

These aspects are illustrated in Diagram 8.

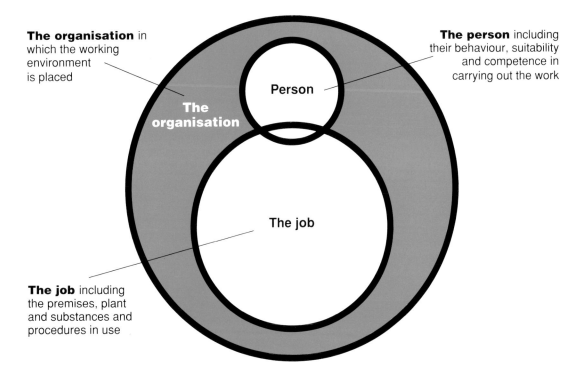

The organisation in which the working environment is placed

The person including their behaviour, suitability and competence in carrying out the work

The organisation

Person

The job

The job including the premises, plant and substances and procedures in use

Diagram 8 Key aspects of investigation

situation and its adequacy (Was it dealt with promptly? Were continuing risks dealt with promptly and adequately? Was the first-aid response adequate? Were emergency procedures followed?);

- whether the event was preventable and how.

The potential consequences

- What was the worst that could have happened?

- What prevented the worst from happening?

- How often could such an event occur (the 'recurrence potential')?

- What was the worst injury or damage which could have resulted (the 'severity potential')?

- How many people could the event have affected (the 'population potential')?

The investigation should consider, in particular, whether the management system was adequate to prevent the event occurring: if not, why not; if so, why did it fail? This involves:

- establishing the circumstances at the time of the event;
- comparing these with the relevant performance standards;
- identifying any inadequacy in the standards or disparity between the standards and the reality; and
- identifying the reasons for any disparity between the reality and the intention.

Results and analysis

The use of standard report forms can help to guide investigators through the processes outlined above. Forms should be large enough to accommodate all the relevant information and should include sufficient space to record clearly the causes of the event and recommended remedial action for each cause. Both the immediate circumstances of the event and the underlying organisational causes should be identified to enable judgements to be made by those responsible for authorising the necessary follow-up action. Forms can also be used as the basis of follow-up procedures to check that all necessary action is taken.

More generally, the recording system must:

- collect information accurately and present it in a consistent form;
- facilitate systematic analysis designed to identify common causes, features and trends which might not be apparent from the investigation of an individual event;
- record information which might foreseeably be needed in the future; it may also be useful for management purposes to record the time taken to undertake investigations and the related costs.

The content of reports may vary according to the type of event, but should generally cover at least the key data identified in Inset 15.

Coding and classification systems may assist in the analysis of collected data. Ideally these systems should provide for the correlation of different variables and analysis of both common features and underlying organisational causes. A number of proprietary computerised accident recording and analysis programmes are available which are designed to meet these requirements. Periodic reviews of report forms should also be undertaken to check that the remedial action identified has been adequate and appropriate.

MEASURING PERFORMANCE
SUMMARY

Organisations achieving success in health and safety measure their performance against pre-determined plans and standards, the implementation and effectiveness of which they assess as a basis for taking appropriate remedial action.

This leads them to establish, operate and maintain systems which ensure that performance is measured objectively. Such systems include:

- active monitoring systems which:
  - measure the achievement of objectives and specified standards;
  - reflect risk control priorities by concentrating on high risk activities which are monitored in more depth and/or more frequently;

- reactive monitoring systems which collect and analyse information suggesting failures in health and safety performance. These require systems for reporting:
  - injuries and cases of ill health;
  - other loss events, eg damage to property;
  - incidents (including all those which had the potential to cause injury, ill health or loss);
  - hazards;
  - weaknesses or omissions in performance standards;

- reporting and response systems which ensure that information from active and reactive monitoring is evaluated by people competent to identify situations which create an immediate risk to health or safety, and to ensure that appropriate remedial action is taken;

- investigation systems which ensure:
  - the investigation of reports arising from active and reactive monitoring, with priority being given to those circumstances which present the greatest risk;
  - the identification of both the immediate and the underlying causes of events;
  - the referral of information to the level of management with authority to initiate the necessary remedial action, including organisational and policy changes;
  - the adequate analysis of all collected data to identify common features or trends and initiate improvements.

FURTHER READING

1 Pilborough L *Inspection of industrial plant: a survey of quality assurance, safety and standards* 2nd edition Gower Technical 1989

2 Ferry TS *Modern accident investigation and analysis* John Wiley & Sons 1988 ISBN 0 471 62481 0

3 HSE *Your firm's injury records and how to use them* free leaflet IND(G) 113L

4 HSE *Surveillance of people exposed to health risks at work: Principles and practice for the surveillance of people exposed to physical, chemical and biological health risks at work* HMSO 1990 HS(G) 61 ISBN 0 11 885574 3

5 *Principles of health and safety at work* IOSH Publishing Ltd 1991 ISBN 0 901357 14 6

6

AUDITING AND REVIEWING PERFORMANCE

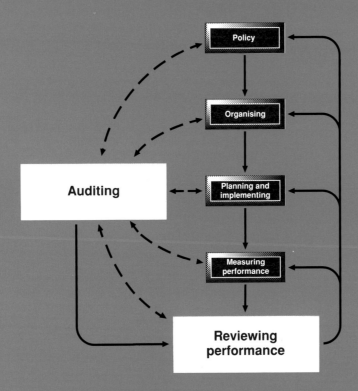

Synopsis

Learning from experience through the use of audits and performance reviews enables organisations achieving high standards of health and safety to maintain and develop their ability to manage risks to the fullest possible extent. This chapter:

- defines the nature and purpose of the health and safety auditing process;

- examines how health and safety performance can be reviewed and what supporting systems are necessary.

AUDITING AND REVIEWING PERFORMANCE

In organisations achieving success in health and safety, reviewing performance is the final step in the health and safety management control cycle. This constitutes the 'feedback loop' needed to enable the organisation to maintain and develop its ability to manage risks to the fullest possible extent. Auditing is also essential to ensure the continued effectiveness of the health and safety management system. As with other aspects of an effective health and safety management system, performance standards for the audit and review process should be established and monitored.

AUDITING

All control systems tend to deteriorate over time or to become obsolete as a result of change. This calls for systems to be regularly audited. Health and safety auditing complements the planning and control cycle and is similar in concept to financial auditing or third-party quality auditing. It aims to provide an independent assessment of the validity and reliability of the management planning and control systems. Auditing supports monitoring by providing managers with information on the implementation and effectiveness of plans and performance standards. It also provides a check on the reliability, efficiency and effectiveness of the arrangements for policy making, organising, planning, implementing, measuring and reviewing performance. Auditing needs to be comprehensive and to examine over time all the components of the health and safety management systems which have been outlined in earlier chapters.

There are various methods of achieving this objective but these can be divided into two different but complementary approaches.

An examination of a 'vertical slice' of activities can be undertaken. This involves examining one specific aspect in each of the elements identified. For example, an audit could be made of the policy on eye protection, fire safety or emergency arrangements. This would involve assessing its adequacy relative to the risks and how effectively the organisation, planning, measuring and reviewing processes secure its implementation.

A 'horizontal slice' approach can also be adopted. In this case one particular element of the safety management system is examined in detail. For example, an in-depth examination could be made of the whole process of planning. Plans could be examined to assess their relevance, how they were formulated and whether they were sufficiently specific and realistic to allow for ready implementation and measurement. In the same way a 'horizontal slice' approach could also be taken in respect of performance standards, examining how they were devised, their relevance to the needs of the organisation and their adequacy (for example, whether those relating to risk control incorporate the correct and up-to-date legal or technical standards; in this case the audit of the system may require a specific technical input).

In practice a combination of vertical and horizontal slice auditing is needed to provide a comprehensive picture of how effectively the health and safety system is controlling risks. This may be undertaken either as a single event or as a rolling programme with different aspects, sections or departments examined in turn. It may involve one or a number of persons. A team approach, involving managers, safety representatives and employees, may be adopted to widen the nature of involvement and co-operation.

In order to maximise the benefit from the auditing process, audits should be conducted by competent people independent of the area or activities being audited. This can be achieved either by using external consultants or by using staff from different sections, departments or sites to audit their colleagues. Organisations may use either their own self-developed auditing system or those marketed as proprietary systems or a combination of both.

HSE supports the use of proprietary systems but does not endorse particular systems. Organisations should decide what system, in-house or proprietary, would best meet its needs taking into account the costs and the potential benefits. In assessing the suitability of proprietary schemes it should be borne in mind that, because of the variability of organisations, it is unlikely that any one system will suit an organisation perfectly. It will generally be necessary to tailor a system to the particular needs of the organisation. Further general advice on the characteristics of effective auditing systems is given in Inset 16.

Audits generate both qualitative and quantitative data on health and safety performance. Many organisations have tried to provide numerical measures to

INSET 16

EFFECTIVE HEALTH AND SAFETY AUDIT SYSTEMS

Effective auditing systems tend to display the following characteristics.

Audits are carried out by competent people who are independent of the area or section being audited. This may involve one person, a team of managers, specialists and non-management employees or external consultants. Those with auditing responsibilities will generally require specific training in this task to secure competence.

Audit systems are designed to assess the following key elements of health and safety management:

- policy - its intent, scope and adequacy;

- the organisation, including:
  - the acceptance of health and safety responsibilities by line managers and the adequacy of arrangements to secure control;
  - the adequacy of the arrangements to secure the involvement of all employees in the health and safety effort;
  - the adequacy of arrangements to secure the communication of policy and relevant information;
  - the adequacy of arrangements to secure the competence of all employees;

- planning and policy implementation including:
  - overall control and direction of the health and safety programme;
  - standard setting - its adequacy and relevance;
  - the allocation of resources to implement standards;
  - the extent of compliance with standards and their effectiveness in risk control;
  - the long-term improvement in the accident and incident performance;

- measuring systems - their adequacy and relevance;

- reviewing systems and the ability of the organisation to learn from experience and improve performance.

quantify audit data so that improvements in performance can be readily measured from year to year. This is a valuable exercise but needs to be supported by sound auditing methodologies which ensure consistency in scoring so that the numerical outputs can be relied upon. Other organisations do not use numerical systems and rely on a purely qualitative approach.

An audit programme should be prepared to complement other health and safety management activities. In the case of offshore installations the Safety Case Regulations 1992, require that the arrangements for audit should be set out in the safety case. Performance standards should be devised for planning and implementing the audit programme and these standards should themselves be monitored. Some organisations have allocated responsibility for health and safety auditing to their existing internal auditing sections in an attempt to fully integrate health and safety management into their existing structures. All audit programmes are only as good as the staff operating them and depend on the imaginative examination and use of the results. Unless they are operated with integrity it is always possible to misuse the system, and checks and balances need to be built in at various levels to prevent this. Such checks and balances are particularly important at the interpretative review stage.

REVIEWING PERFORMANCE

Reviewing is the process concerned with making judgements about the adequacy of performance and taking decisions about the nature and timing of the actions necessary to remedy deficiencies. In common with all health and safety management activities, suitable performance standards should be established to identify the responsibilities, timing and systems of reviewing. Supporting performance standards and systems are also necessary to track the implementation of those decisions arising from the review process.

The speed and nature of the response to any situation should be determined by the degree of risk involved and the availability of resources. The application of risk assessment principles outlined in chapter 4 contributes to decision making by assisting the identification of risk priorities. The effectiveness of review systems is in part determined by the competence of those involved and people responsible for making review decisions should receive specific training in making this type of judgement.

The general aims of the review process reflect the objectives of the planning process, and are to secure:
- the maintenance and development of health and safety policy;
- the maintenance and development of an effective organisation with a positive health and safety culture; and
- the maintenance and development of performance standards and reporting systems for controlling both the health and safety systems and specific risks.

The effectiveness of review activities is enhanced by:
- clearly establishing who is responsible for implementing the remedial action identified in the review process;
- setting deadlines for the completion of remedial action.

Reviewing performance is based on information from measuring activities (including both active and reactive monitoring) and from auditing activities in which an independent assessment is made of the whole safety management system.

Reviewing the results of internal measuring activities is a continuous process which is undertaken at various levels within an organisation. It includes, for example:
- responses by first line supervisors to remedy failures to implement performance standards which they observe in the course of routine activities;
- responses to remedy specific examples of substandard performance which are identified by reactive monitoring;
- responses to remedy examples of substandard performance identified as a result of active monitoring; and
- responses to the assessment of plans and objectives either at individual, departmental, site, group or organisational level.

The reviews undertaken in the first two cases occur randomly and cannot be planned. It is, however, important that review procedures are consistently applied in these cases. The reviews in the last two cases should arise from planned monitoring activities and should be controlled by appropriate performance standards. They may, for example, include:
- monthly reviews of individual supervisors or sections;
- three monthly reviews of departments;
- annual reviews of sites or of the organisation as a whole.

Organisations must decide on the frequency of reviews at each level and the design of review activities should be tailored to the measuring activities discussed in the last chapter. Similarly, decisions need to be made on how to review the audit data and integrate it into the general review procedures.

Successful organisations use a number of key performance indicators relating to overall performance and the management of improvements as the basis for reviews at the highest level. While each organisation needs to develop its own indicators, it is suggested that at least the following four indicators should be involved:
- assessment of the degree of compliance with performance standards;
- identification of areas where performance standards are absent or inadequate (those areas where further action is necessary to develop the total health and safety management system);
- assessment of the achievement of specific objectives; and
- accident, ill health and incident data, accompanied by analyses of both the immediate and underlying causes, trends and common features.

The process of feeding information on success and failure back into the system is an essential element in motivating employees to improve performance. Successful organisations emphasise positive reinforcement and concentrate on encouraging progress on those indicators which demonstrate improvements in risk control.

In addition to making internal assessments of their achievements, organisations may 'bench-mark' their performance against other organisations. This generally takes two forms:
- comparing accident rates with those of organisations in the same industry who use similar production processes and experience similar risks (Appendix 4 provides further information on the calculation and use of

accident incidence and frequency rates); and

· comparing management practices and techniques with those of organisations in any industry, so as to provide a wide perspective and gain new insights on the management of similar problems.

As part of a demonstration of corporate responsibilities some organisations are also now accounting for their health and safety performance in their published annual reports. Increasingly organisations are prepared and able to identify not only the efforts put into health and safety but also the result of this in terms of improved health and safety performance and reductions in avoidable costs.

AUDITING AND REVIEWING PERFORMANCE
SUMMARY

Organisations achieving success in health and safety aim to evaluate performance, in order to:
- maximise learning and to ensure that appropriate action is taken to improve the control of specific risks; and
- to improve overall health and safety performance and further develop their health and safety policies.

This leads them to establish, operate and maintain audit and review systems which ensure that:

- information is obtained by the use of in-house auditing systems or external auditors on the validity and reliability of the whole health and safety management planning and control system, and the ability of the organisation to develop its health and safety policies and improve the control of risks;

- appropriate remedial action is taken to deal with specific issues arising from measurement activities and to ensure that progress in implementing remedial action is followed through according to plan;

- the overall effectiveness of policy implementation is assessed internally with particular reference to the following four key performance indicators:
  - assessments of the degree of compliance with health and safety performance standards;
  - identification of areas where standards are absent or inadequate;
  - assessment of the achievement of specific objectives;
  - accident, ill health and incident data together with analyses of immediate and underlying causes, trends and common features;

- health and safety performance is assessed externally by comparison with other organisations.

FURTHER READING

1 Camp RC *Bench marking: the search for industry best practices that lead to superior performance* Quality Press 1989 ISBN 0 87389 058 2.

2 Kase DW and Wiese KJ *Safety auditing: a management tool* Van Nostrand Reinhold 1990 ISBN 0 44 223746 4

3 HSE *A guide to the Offshore Installations (Safety Case) Regulations 1992* 1992 HMSO ISBN 0 11 882055 9

4 HSE *Work equipment* Guidance on Regulations 1992 HMSO ISBN 0 11 886332 0

5 HSE *Manual handling* Guidance on Regulations 1992 HMSO ISBN 0 11 886335 5

6 HSC *Workplace health, safety and welfare* Approved Code of Practoce 1992 HMSO ISBN 0 11 886333 9

7 HSE *Personal protective equipment at work* Guidance on Regulations 1992 HMSO, ISBN 0 11 886334 7

8 HSE *Display screen equipment work* Guidance on Regulations 1992 HMSO ISBN 0 11 886331 2

9 HSC *Management of health and safety at work* Approved Code of Practice 1992 HMSO ISBN 0 11 886330 4

Appendices

Appendix 1

TERMINOLOGY

In this publication:

Policy is used in relation to health and safety and other functional management areas, (eg manufacturing and human resources) to convey the general intentions, approach and objectives of an organisation and the criteria and principles on which actions and responses are based. The term, 'written policy statements' is used to describe those documents which record the policy of the organisation.

Organisation is used as a general term to describe the responsibilities and relationships between individuals which forms the social environment in which work takes place. **Organising** is regarded as the process of designing and establishing these responsibilities and relationships. The expression 'statements of organisation' is used to describe those documents which record those responsibilities and relationships.

Organisation is also used to refer to any undertaking subject to the Health and Safety at Work etc Act 1974. Including:
- companies and firms in the extractive, manufacturing, construction agricultural, transport and service industries;
- commercial and financial institutions, such as banks, building societies and insurance companies;
- public utilities and institutions, such as the health service, research laboratories, colleges, universities and local authorities;
- non-profit making institutions, such as charities.

Accident includes any undesired circumstances which give rise to ill health or injury; damage to property, plant, products or the environment; production losses, or increased liabilities.

Incident includes all undesired circumstances and near misses which have the potential to cause accidents.

Hazard means the potential to cause harm, including ill health and injury; damage to property, plant, products or the environment; production losses or increased liabilities.

Ill health includes acute and chronic ill health caused by physical, chemical or biological agents as well as adverse effects on mental health.

Risk means the likelihood that a specified undesired event will occur due to the realisation of a hazard by, or during, work activities or by the products and services created by work activities.

Planning is used to describe the process by which the objectives and methods of implementing the health and safety policy are decided. It is concerned with allocating resources (eg money, time or effort) to achieve objectives and decide priorities. It ranges from general topics dealing with the direction of the whole organisation to detailed issues concerned with standard setting and the control of specific risks.

Measuring means the collection of information about the implementation and effectiveness of plans and standards. This involves a variety of checking or 'monitoring' activities.

Auditing is the structured process of collecting independent information on the efficiency, effectiveness and reliability of the total safety management system and drawing up plans for corrective action.

Reviewing is used to describe activities involving judgements about performance, and decisions about improving performance. Reviewing is based on information from 'measuring' and 'auditing' activities.

Appendix 2
ORGANISING FOR HEALTH AND SAFETY

Key tasks for policy makers, planners and implementers of policy

The key tasks of **policy makers** include:
- devising health and safety policy;
- establishing strategies to implement policy and integrating these into general business activity;
- specifying a structure for planning, measuring, reviewing and auditing health and safety policy;
- specifying a structure for implementing policy and supporting plans;
- agreeing plans for improvement and reviewing progress to develop both the organisation and the policy;
- pursuing health and safety objectives with evident sincerity.

The major outputs of **policy makers** include:
- written statements of general health and safety policy and strategic objectives;
- written statements of the organisation for planning, measuring, reviewing and auditing;
- written statements of the organisation for implementation;
- general plans containing specific objectives for each year.

The key tasks of **planners** include:
- producing detailed plans to achieve corporate health and safety objectives;
- establishing performance standards for planning, measuring, reviewing and auditing health and safety policy implementation;
- co-ordinating the specialist advice which is necessary to ensure effective planning and implementation of policy, for example, the input of health and safety specialists, engineers, architects and doctors;
- ensuring the participation and involvement of workers in compliance with the Health and Safety at Work etc Act Sections 2(6) and (7) and the Safety Representatives and Safety Committees Regulations 1977;
- keeping up-to-date with changes in health and safety legislation, standards and good practice and with management practices relevant to the organisation.

The key outputs of **planners** include:
- health and safety strategy statements and plans to support the policy;
- health and safety operational plans which identify specific health and safety objectives to be achieved within fixed time periods;
- performance standards and supporting systems and procedures;
- up-to-date documentation of plans, performance standards and systems.

The key tasks for **implementers** are:
- implementation of operational plans, performance standards, systems and procedures and the provision of necessary physical and human resources and information;
- provision of timely feedback on performance including successes and failures and any deficiencies in plans, standards, procedures and systems;
- ensuring participation at all levels in health and safety activities.

The key outputs of **implementers** are:
- safe and healthy production and delivery of products and services;
- products and services which in themselves do not create risks to others.

Appendix 3
MINIMUM OBJECTIVES FOR PERFORMANCE STANDARDS

FIRST STAGE - CONTROL OF INPUTS

Design and selection of premises

Performance standards should ensure that:
- appropriate health and safety aspects of the proposed use, other foreseeable uses and future maintenance of premises are included in the design, selection and purchase plans and specifications;
- health and safety aspects of construction are considered at the design stage to ensure that construction takes place in accordance with best health and safety practice and that the health and safety of direct employees and contractors' staff is achieved;
- health and safety standards are detailed in contract specifications and that compliance with these is checked during the course of construction work.

Design and selection of plant and substances

Performance standards should ensure that:
- all relevant health and safety aspects, including technical standards and human factors issues, relating to installation, use, maintenance, decommissioning, dismantling and disposal are considered at the design stage and incorporated into design specifications;
- all design specifications refer to health and safety requirements, including relevant aspects of human factors, and that these are specified in all contract documents;
- all relevant health and safety data is collected when plant and substances are being selected for purchase;
- health and safety performance is considered in the selection of suppliers;
- all relevant health and safety requirements are specified in all purchase order documents;
- procedures for the receipt and storage of goods ensure that only plant and substances which satisfy the health and safety specifications in the order are accepted.

Plant and substances used by others

Performance standards should ensure that:
- initial and ongoing checks of plant and substances used by contractors are adequate to ensure that their design, formulation and use is consistent with the on-site policy and standards.

Acquisitions

Performance standards should ensure that:
- health and safety standards and loss potential are considered in business purchase decisions. Where feasible this should involve a full assessment of existing management systems; of the health and safety record, including the potential for forward loss; and of on-site conditions.

Human resources

Performance standards should ensure that:
- employees are recruited on the basis of selection criteria which include reference to relevant physical and mental abilities;

- these selection criteria are based on assessments and health and safety analysis of job requirements;
- health and safety performance is considered when awarding contracts and that this includes assessments of:
  - safety policy and the safety management system;
  - health and safety performance on previous contracts;
  - accident, ill health and incident records; and
  - compliance with health and safety policy.

Information inputs

Performance standards should ensure that:
- all relevant information concerning legislation, standards and general management practice is gathered, drawn to the attention of those with a particular interest, and made available to all others who may express an interest.

SECOND STAGE - CONTROL OF WORK ACTIVITIES

Performance standards for organisational control

Control

Performance standards should establish and maintain the necessary organisation and procedures for:
- policy formulation and development;
- organisation design and development;
- planning, measuring, auditing and reviewing performance.

Co-operation

Performance standards should ensure:
- the continued informed involvement of all work people and, where appropriate, secure compliance with the Safety Representatives and Safety Committee Regulations 1977 and the Offshore Installations (Safety Representatives and Safety Committee) Regulations 1989.

Communication

Performance standards should:
- facilitate the creation and flow of all essential information throughout the organisation.

Competence

Performance standards should ensure that all employees are competent in the health and safety aspects of their work and include reference to:
- an assessment of suitability before recruitment and placement;
- the provision of training and supervision to ensure competence;
- health surveillance and monitoring.

Performance standards for risk control

Performance standards should ensure that risks are eliminated where possible or, if not eliminated, are adequately controlled in order of priority by suitable physical means, by systems of work or protective equipment.

In establishing performance standards for risk control, consideration should be given to the following issues:

- The operation of the productive system in the 'steady state', including routine and non-routine activities, on-site storage and the transport, handling and use of plant, equipment and substances;
- Maintenance of the system in the 'steady state' including health and safety aspects of the maintenance work itself, whether undertaken in-house or by contractors;
- Planned change from the 'steady state' arising from changes in premises, plant and substances, procedures, people or information. The standards should identify all foreseeable changes, evaluate the health and safety implications and, where appropriate, plan for change so as to cater for health and safety.
- Foreseeable emergencies (such as fire, injuries, ill health incidents and the failure of key control equipment, power sources or services). The standards should cover:
  - identification of all foreseeable emergencies by a systematic survey and analysis;
  - responsibilities for emergency planning and disaster control;
  - arrangements for personnel evacuation and the provision of first aid;
  - the procedures for disaster control and management and for rescue by employees or the emergency services, if appropriate;
  - arrangements for the rehearsal of emergency procedures.

THIRD STAGE - CONTROL OF OUTPUTS

Products and services

Performance standards should ensure that:

- products are designed and developed to ensure health and safety in use, storage and transport;
- the design of services secures health and safety in their provision;
- the necessary research is undertaken into the health and safety of the use of products and services;
- arrangements are made for the packaging, labelling and intermediate storage to ensure health and safety in delivery and transport;
- arrangements are made for health and safety in the installation, setting up, cleaning and maintenance of products.

By-products of work activities

Performance standards should ensure:

- that risks to others who may be affected are considered during the planning and control of all activities, including the manufacture and delivery of products and the provision of services;
- adequate and appropriate control of unwanted outputs, such as wastes and atmospheric emissions.

Information for external use

Performance standards should ensure:

- the compilation of information concerning product and service safety in connection with purchase, use, maintenance, transport, handling, storage and disposal;
- the compilation and distribution of information relevant to non-employees who may be affected by work activities, such as members of the public, other employers and their employees, emergency services and planning authorities.

Appendix 4
ACCIDENT INCIDENCE AND FREQUENCY RATES

Accident incidence and frequency rates provide a means of measuring safety performance over time and comparing it with accident statistics published by external sources, such as the Health and Safety Executive (HSE).

Employers have to keep records of injuries at work and report certain types to the appropriate enforcing authority, usually HSE or a local authority*. Reportable injuries include fatal and major injuries to employees, self-employed people and members of the public, and injuries that cause incapacity for work for more than three days to employees and self-employed people ('over-3-day injuries'). Statistical information from these injury reports is collated by HSE and published in the Health and Safety Commission's annual report and as an annual supplement to the *Employment Gazette*. The published information gives details of injuries reported from each major sector of industry as classified by the 1980 Standard Industrial Classification.

The accuracy of the nationally collated injury statistics depends on employers complying with the legal reporting requirements. In some industries under reporting of injuries by employers is a serious problem. Firms with good record keeping arrangements in an industry with a high level of under-reporting may therefore find that their injury rates compare unfavourably with the published rates for their industry. The figures in such cases obviously must be interpreted accordingly. Incidence rates can, however, still be used to monitor performance over time and between different departments.

Calculation of injury incidence rates
Comparing reportable injury information is just one way of assessing a firm's safety performance. In many firms, particularly those with fewer than 100 employees, reportable injuries represent only a small proportion of the total number of injuries to employees. Records of more minor, non-reportable injuries, and of 'near misses', may also be converted into incidence rates and used to monitor trends over time or between different parts of the operation. Analysis of the data to identify the main causes of injury, for example, can help to identify risks that need to be controlled and prevent further accidents.

Calculation of injury incidence rates
HSE's formula for calculating an annual injury incidence rate is:

$$\frac{\text{Number of reportable injuries in financial year}}{\text{Average number employed during year}} \quad \text{x} \quad 100\,000$$

This gives the rate per 100 000 employees. The formula makes no allowance for variations in part-time employment or overtime. It is an annual calculation and the figures need to be adjusted pro-rata if they cover a shorter period. Such shorter term rates should be compared only with rates for exactly similar periods - not the national annual rates.

---

* The reporting requirements are contained in the Reporting of Injuries, Diseases and Dangerous Occurrences Regulations 1985 (RIDDOR) and are described in a HSE guide to the Regulations, HS(R)23, available from HMSO.

Calculation of injury frequency rates

While HSE calculates injury *incidence* rates per 100 000 employees, some parts of industry prefer to calculate injury *frequency* rates, usually per million hours worked. This method, by counting hours worked rather than the number of employees, avoids distortions which may be caused in the incidence rate calculations by part and full time employees and by overtime working. Frequency rates can be calculated for any time period.

The calculation is:

$$\frac{\text{Number of injuries in the period}}{\text{Total hours worked during the period}} \quad \text{x} \quad 1\ 000\ 000$$

(Further information on accident incidence and frequency rates is contained in the HSE publication *Your firm's injury records and how to use them* - see page 56, reference 3.)

Printed and published by the Health and Safety Executive   C100   10/93

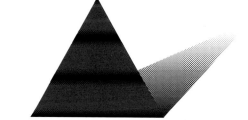